From the Octagon
people • places • news • views

Also by Allen Young

Out of the Closets: Voices of Gay Liberation, editor with Karla Jay, Douglas-Links Books, 1972; NYU Press, 1992.

After You're Out: Personal Experiences of Gay Men and Lesbian Women editor with Karla Jay, Links Books, 1974.

Gay Sunshine Interview, with Allen Ginsberg, Grey Fox Press, 1974.

Lavender Culture, editor with Karla Jay, Jove Books, 1979; NYU Press, 1994.

The Gay Report with Karla Jay, Summit Books, 1977.

Gays Under the Cuban Revolution, Grey Fox Press, 1981.

More Than Sand and Sea: Images of Cape Cod, editor, with wood engravings by G. Brender á Brandis, The Brandstead Press, 1982; Millers River Publishing Co., 1985.

North of Quabbin: A Guide to Nine Massachusetts Towns, Millers River Publishing Co., 1983.

The Millers River Reader, editor; Millers River Publishing Co., 1987.

North of Quabbin Revisited: A Guide to Nine Massachusetts Towns North of Quabbin Reservoir, Haley's, 2003.

Erving Paper Mills Centennial, Erving Paper Mills, 2005.

Twenty Years, Twenty Hikes: A Guide to Twenty Hikes on Protected Land in North Central Massachusetts, with John Burk and Elizabeth Farnsworth, Mount Grace Land Conservation Trust, 2007.

Make Hay While the Sun Shines: Farms, Forests and People of the North Quabbin, iUniverse, Inc., 2007.

Thalassa: One Week in a Provincetown Dune Shack, Haley's, 2011.

The Man Who Got Lost: North Quabbin Stories, Haley's, 2013.

Left, Gay & Green: A Writer's Life, Create Space, 2018.

From the Octagon
people • places
news • views
Allen Young

Haley's
Athol, Massachusetts

© 2025 by Allen Young

All rights reserved. With the exception of short excerpts in a review or critical article, no part of this book may be re-produced by any means, including information storage and retrieval or photocopying equipment, without written permission of the publisher, Haley's.

Haley's
488 South Main Street
Athol, MA 01331
haley.antique@verizon.net • 978.249.9400

Copy edited by Debra Ellis.

Cover photo by Mike Phillips.

Articles reprinted with permission of
Newspapers of Massachusetts for selections from
    Athol Daily News
        and
New Journalism Project for selections from
    Rag Blog

Thanks to the *Christian Science Monitor* and
    Uniquely Quabbin magazine, where the author
    retains copyright

International Standard Book Number: 978-1-956055-36-8

Library of Congress Catalog Number: pending

Dedication

for people everywhere striving for community,

social justice, peace, democracy,

and a healthy planet Earth

Contents

Writing from the Octagon House 1
   an introduction by Allen Young

People

Casey Williams Comes Home
   to Pursue Music and Art 7
Royalston Couple Lives
   with Thirty-Three Cats 11
Dale Monette Presents Wildlife and
   Scenic Photography 15
At Ninety-four, Jerry Chiasson
   Is Still Drumming 19
Meet My New Neighbor, Jesse Rix,
   a Tattoo Artist 23
Love, Adventure, Community
   Define a Couple's Life 28
Kathy Morris, Scientist/Librarian,
   Wheat Weaver 32
Maureen Blasco, Unsung Hero of Royalston . . . 36
At Eighty-seven, Jack Borden
   Continues to Look at the Sky 40
Paul McGinnis: A Lifetime as
   Logger, Teamster, and Sawyer 44
Betty Kimball of Orange Is Really Good
   at Restoring Old Homes 47
Local Women on Motorcycles Travel . . . .
   to Motor Maids' Gathering 51

continued on page viii

Dynamic Well-Known Athol Couple
   Leaving for Arizona........................ 55
Chris Donelan: A Progressive Sheriff
   Begins His Work 60
Robert Perkins, Newspaper Techie,
   is Retiring................................ 64
Meet Walker Korby
   of Trustees of Reservations................ 68
Congressman Jim McGovern:
   A Passionate Man 72
Athol's Last Iceman Shares Some Memories... 76
Remembering Joyce O'Lari, Veteran
   Athol Daily News Reporter 80
Two Local Artists:
   Michael Humphries and Ami Fagin......... 86
Meet Nellie Melaika,
   Grand Dame of Athol's Lithuanians......... 90
A Backhoe, a Bulldozer, and
   Many Stories to Tell 94
Noteworthy Visual Artists
   Tom Kellner and Linda Ruel Flynn 98
Royalston Assessor Gets Assessed
   on the High Side 103
Duo Travels to Alaska and Back
   on a Harley-Davidson Road King 107
Remembering Gene Bishop and Herman Goldfarb,
   Two Doctors and Activists for Peace........ 111
Discretion, Valor, and the "Good Liberal" 123
The Strange Short Life of Minerva Mayo..... 125
Dental Hygienist Lynn Trinque
   Is a Dedicated Professional............... 129

Shrewsbury Native Dan Zona,
    North Quabbin Leader 133
Is a Muralist a Contortionist? An Acrobat?
    Read About It Here 137
At Seventy, Petersham's Larry Buell
    Maintains His Environmental Vision. 142
Abbey Plotkin: Her Good Heart Gave Out 146
My Strange Aunt Sylvia 149

Places

A Visit to Provincetown..................... 163
A Ten-Day Visit to Pennsylvania 167
Monkeys, Birds, Beaches, People, and Planes:
    A Trip to Costa Rica 171
Mead and Beneski:
    A Visit to Two Museums in Amherst 175
Creating a Meadow to Encourage Biodiversity. . 179
Small Monuments Found In Many Places.... 184
Two Unique Villages:
    Tully and North Leverett 190
Sleepy River Town in Brazil 195

News

A Peek into the Massachusetts................
    Legalized Cannabis Business 203
Workers Credit Union's Rich History
    Linked to Immigrants 214
A Deadly Disease Hits the North Quabbin:
    Heroin Addiction 218
Two Antique Ladies Visit an Antique House. . 223
Federal Anti-Lynching Law Passed At Last .. 227
Millions React to the Beginning
    of the Trump Era....................... 232

continued on page x

Views

Vermont Nuke Is Old.
   It's Time to Shut it Down 239
In Defense of Drag Queens 242
Solar Arrays Should Not Be Built
   Just Anywhere......................... 253
A Gilded-Age Mansion in Orange
   on Sale for $742,500 256
Let's Reinvigorate
   the North Quabbin Bioreserve 260
Who Is Athol's Most Famous Native Son 264
Ethel Rosenberg's Life Story
   Told in New Book...................... 267
Appreciating Nature as a Political Act....... 277
Acknowledgments 283
About the Author 285
Colophon................................ 289

Writing from the Octagon House
an introduction by Allen Young

For about a half century, the unique eight-sided building on the cover of *From the Octagon* has been my home. I call it, simply, the Octagon House, part of the Butterworth Farm intentional community on a gravel country road founded in 1973 in the town of Royalston, Massachusetts, population 1,200.

The Octagon House is where I eat, drink, sleep, laugh, cry, listen to the radio, watch TV, go on the internet, make phone calls, get stoned, make love, have fun, celebrate, worry, stress out, relax and try to remain healthy as I age. I am eighty-four years old and essentially retired from the working world after being a professional writer since my youth. After decades of maintaining a prolific vegetable garden, I also quit gardening a few years ago, thus succumbing to a combination of old age and sloth.

On the top floor of the Octagon House, I have written hundreds of articles and authored or edited a dozen books. In recent years, most of my published work consisted of a weekly *Athol Daily News* column, which I called "Inside/Outside." I gave up the column but write occasionally for a blog—self-described as "the latest in news and views from the progressive front." Called the *Rag Blog* and produced by old friends involved in the underground press—as I was—in the 1960s, the blog originates in Austin, Texas. I have included several pieces from the *Rag Blog* in *From the Octagon.*

As explained, I've entitled the book *From the Octagon.* I've subtitled it *People, Places, News, Views.* Although some readers who like the human interest articles in the People section may not appreciate my opinions in the Views section, the totality of the compilation expresses my interests, values, and life details.

For more about Butterworth Farm, construction of the Octagon House, and my life as a writer and activist, I recommend my autobiography *Left, Gay & Green: A Writer's Life* published in 2018 by Create Space. Readers will find it available from booksellers and in many libraries, including through inter-library loan in Massachusetts.

From the Octagon is an anthology, a collection of articles, most published during the fifteen years since 2010. A few are older, and some have never been published before. In most of the writing, I use journalistic skills learned over many decades from teachers, editors, and life experience. One might say I have natural talent as a writer much as people have natural talent as athletes and musicians. Although I lack athletic or musical talent, I appreciate and admire those who do.

I hope you enjoy *From the Octagon.* Feel welcome to contact me by email at allenyoung355@gmail.com, and I am likely to respond.

People

Casey Williams Comes Home to Pursue Music and Art
2017

Casey Williams
photo courtesy of Casey Williams

She studied, worked, made friends, and had fun in Amherst. Then she did the same in Boston, but after almost two decades of being away, Casey Williams came home to Athol and has no regrets.

"I found it to be so calm and peaceful here, and that seemed much more important than going to a funky sushi place," she said. The return to the North Quabbin region has opened new creative doorways for this trained, talented forty-one-year-old artist.

It started with a nine-town North Quabbin region map, not a commercial-style map but an artistic painting, and continued with similar but much more detailed painting-maps of about thirty towns and communities.

Casey also continues her career, launched in Boston, as a disc jockey, using the moniker Just Joan DJ.

With curly golden locks reminiscent of Botticelli paintings, Casey defined herself as an artist early in life. She said, "Painting is at my core" and remembers being influenced by the Athol High School art curriculum of teacher Tina Hause.

Casey is a 1993 AHS grad, and her return to the area includes residing with her father, Tom Williams.

Following graduation, Casey enrolled at UMass, Amherst, living in dorms. She recounts, "I immediately felt swallowed up by UMass. My entire AHS class had ninety kids, and some of my individual classes at UMass had ninety! I didn't love it, though I liked being in Amherst.

"I stayed in school for three semesters, then continued in the town. I liked being social there, just having fun, exploring, and being out of Athol, which seemed so small and contained when I was growing up. I supported myself by waitressing and cleaning, taking little jobs to afford living in an apartment with some girlfriends. But after two years, I felt the need to get back into school."

Introduced by Tina Hause to the School of the Museum of Fine Arts in Boston, Casey enrolled there and obtained a bachelor's degree in fine arts. By chance, she made her home in Jamaica Plain, a neighborhood that I associate with friends rooted in the 1960s New Left and counterculture. Casey said she was "oblivious to that, but I quickly realized that this was a very comfortable place for me, with an underground scene—funky, artsy." She started waiting tables at Bella Luna, a restaurant upstairs from the Milky Way Lounge and Lanes, a bowling alley and party place with a dance floor.

One night, a DJ didn't show up, and Casey gave it a try. There were other DJs in town named Casey, so she took the name Just Joan after Joan Wilder, a favorite kooky movie character.

Casey's mom, Ann Williams, AHS guidance director, became gravely ill, and that's what brought Casey back home. Ann died in 2011. Casey was bereft and worked with Marcia Gagliardi of Haley's to publish a book entitled *Dawn's Agenda,* a collection of her mother's poems, available on Amazon.com. Each poem is paired with an illustration by Casey.

She became curious about the concept of the North Quabbin region, and that led to her map illustrations. Their complexity is intriguing. The Athol map, for example, has a beautiful image of a thistle symbolizing the town's Scottish roots plus a Starrett micrometer, ponds and streams, a River Rat cartoon, and a dozen other details.

Casey commented, "Paintings are free and more expressive of who I am. Maps are more pragmatic, but I do love what the maps create, engaging with people, connecting with the community." She welcomes commissioned customized maps—for example, a couple in Barre acquired her town map printed on a card with a white dot to show the wedding location.

Casey loves being back home and reports, "I feel like I am making more artwork now than I ever have. I'm away from the rat race, and there's less stress."

She recalls, "My mother on her death bed said, 'Do what makes you truly happy. Don't worry about anything else.'"

Casey is also on the team creating the *Uniquely Quabbin* magazine, with the third issue due out shortly. My article about architecture is in it. Just Joan the DJ continues to work, too.

Email justjoandj@gmail for art including maps and DJ inquiries.

I'll conclude this column with a few words from Marcia Gagliardi, who introduced me to Casey:

A light-hearted but disciplined artist with a competent hand and sure eye, Casey turns out original work that appeals to collectors at all levels. Casey's mom and I worked together at Athol High School for many years, and we each had three daughters of similar spacing and age.

Ann had a fantabulous sense of humor and creative turn of mind, and during AHS Spirit Weeks, she engineered our dressing in the same outrageous costumes. Once we dressed as nuns, and Ann Killay (chair of the selectboard who ran a stationery store in town) called us Sister Britannica and Sister Scholastica.

Ann suggested Athol Area YMCA Swim Team for the Gagliardi girls, so the Williamses and Gagliardis often hung out together at practices and after-meet debriefings over something good to eat. The families often socialized together. Casey and her sisters and her dad remain close to my heart, and like Ann, they are generous, creative, spirited, and hard-working. I am very lucky that they are part of my life.

Published in *Athol Daily News,* January 19, 2017
Copyright © 2017 by Newspapers of Massachusetts, Inc.
Used with permission.

Royalston Couple Lives with Thirty-Three Cats
2014

Stephanie and John McClure live in the center of Royalston with their thirty-three cats. Sure, that's a lot of cats, but at one point they had forty-five! Caring for many cats with affection and dedication has been a central part of the McClures' lives for decades.

Cats gather on a rug in the McClure home
photo courtesy of Stephanie McClure

I'm aware there are a few other people in the North Quabbin region who have a comparable number of felines, but I decided to focus only on the McClures here. In case you are wondering, I have had no pets for many years, and the most cats I have ever owned at one time is two.

The McClures were in their 60s when I interviewed them, but cats became important to the McClures' lives in the early years of their relationship. They were in their twenties when they got married and were living in Virginia, as John was a United States Park Police officer working in the District of Columbia.

Following John's retirement, the couple moved in 1992 to Royalston, where Stephanie's parents, the late Pat and John Poor, were living.

Dogs as well as cats are beloved by the McClures, and they have had as many as eight Chow Chows. Now, they have two Newfoundlands.

Stephanie recalled that the family had Siamese cats in her childhood and were even able to travel with them to distant lands due to her father's career as a US Navy officer.

She added, "When John and I were first married, people used to bring cats to our house. I even got a cat that was seized in a drug bust one time, brought in by a police officer I had never seen before."

Some of the cats they've taken into their home were feral, living outdoors, and often suffering. The oldest cat in the house now, a fifteen-year-old female, was taken in from the wild. Stephanie was once notified about a feral cat that had eight kittens, but the unfortunate mother compelled six of them to a certain death, as she was aware that she could feed only two.

Of the thirty-three cats in the McClure home, only four are allowed outside. The others are assigned to certain rooms in the house, with as many as seven allowed to sleep in Stephanie's bed. Seventeen stay "upstairs in a cat room" which includes window perches and a climbing tree.

Asked about what she likes about cats, Stephanie said, "I like pretty much everything, except the litter box part. There is something very soothing about stroking a cat that's purring, that's warm, but not all are snuggle bunnies, of course. There are several who sleep under the covers with me. Cats are mysterious, and each one has its own personality. Some are very talkative, and others never make a sound."

As for litter, there are approximately eighteen litterboxes in different areas of the house. Stephanie uses both clay litter and the "scoopable clumping stuff." Cats have their preferences about which litter box to use, and all the litter boxes require daily emptying and washing. The waste is taken to the town transfer station, ending up in a landfill.

Asked about odor, Stephanie said, "I'm not sure I would notice."

The couple has no children, and they do not entertain visitors. Stephanie explained, "A lot of people are not comfortable around cats. They're just everywhere. It's hard to keep a place clean or neat. We never go away together except maybe a couple of hours at a time, though John goes often to volunteer at a dog shelter in Baldwinville."

All of the cats have been neutered, and any that become sick are taken to a veterinarian for care. Since around 2001, the couple has used Dr. Andy Cooke of Troy, New Hampshire, to care for sick cats and to euthanize individuals, sometimes several in one year. Stephanie believes that quality of life for her felines is more important than longevity.

Veterinary care, food and litter cost the McClures from two thousand dollars to three thousand dollars a month.

Stephanie realizes her "hobby" of caring for many cats is "very expensive and very restricting," and she would like to downsize her cat population to about a dozen. She now says a firm "no" to anyone approaching them to take in a new cat and refers such people to local shelters.

Published in *Athol Daily News,* April 24, 2014
Copyright © 2014 by Newspapers of Massachusetts, Inc.
Used with permission.

UPDATE
The McClures no longer have a large number of cats.

Dale Monette Presents Wildlife and Scenic Photography 2016

Dale Monette takes time to enjoy the outdoors in Canada.
photo courtesy of Dale Monette

There were no rattlesnakes or any other snakes in Dale Monette's "Quabbin Seasons and Wildlife" photography presentation at the Wendell Public Library, but the brightly colored closeups of painted turtles represented the reptile category quite well.

Dale, like his childhood friend Dave Small, is a retired Massachusetts Department of Conservation and

Recreation, DCR, employee as well as a dedicated birder and wildlife photographer. Dave and Dale were both influenced by the late Robert Coyle, junior high school science teacher and founder of the Athol Bird and Nature Club.

Not long ago, such a photo display was called a slide show, but slides are mostly a thing of the past. The images are shot with a digital Nikon camera, stored on a computer, and projected onto a screen. I saw bald eagles and more warblers than I knew existed in our region and many waterfowl including blue herons, loons, and lots of different ducks with interesting shapes and colors. In the category of mammals, Dale captured images of moose, deer, beavers, and the elusive otter.

Wendell's relatively new library building features the pleasant Herrick Room for presentations such as Dale's. Library director Rosie Heidcamp presided over a full house and introduced Dale, who lives in neighboring New Salem with his wife, Sharon Tracy, the head of Quabbin Mediation in Orange.

Dale's printed photographs, nicely framed and placed around the room, were displayed for two months. Wendell friends Julia Rabin and Dick Baldwin helped mount the exhibition. Dale presented his show also for the Athol Bird and Nature Club monthly meeting in the Millers River Environmental Center and at the Quabbin Visitor Center at Winsor Dam, Belchertown.

Introducing Dale's work for the Town of Wendell website, Dick Baldwin wrote:

> Wildlife photography is a difficult process to say the least. In addition to knowing how to handle digital camera equipment, the photographer must deal with being in the right place at the right time. Dale depends on his skills as

an outdoors man to know about the habits of birds and animals in their environment, to understand the relationship between weather and wildlife activity, and to manage the relationship between himself and his subjects.

Dale prides himself on using powerful telephoto lenses so he doesn't have to disturb the creatures he is admiring and photographing. He thinks bothering them would just be wrong. There are some inconveniences to his work, including getting up early in the morning, tolerating uncomfortable forest and swamp conditions, and patience—lots of patience.

Dale's employment situation changed dramatically in the 1980s with the closing of the Litton Industries, formerly Union Twist Drill plant in Athol. He had been a factory worker there and suddenly had to reconsider his pathway in life. He earned a degree from UMass, Amherst, and with a strong interest in nature, worked for the state's Division of Fisheries and Wildlife before transferring to the DCR.

Dale spent much time in remote areas of the Quabbin helping scientists with environmental studies. He participated in many projects covered on the front page of the *Athol Daily News*, including warmly welcomed bald eagle restoration and controversial launching of a deer hunt in the Quabbin.

He interacted with the public for many years at the Quabbin Visitors Center, developing a relaxed and often humorous approach that made his Wendell show almost as much fun as watching otters playing in the wild. When he retired in 2014, he knew he wanted to return to the Quabbin interior with camera in hand. His photography mentors included Jack Swedberg and Bill Byrne of Massachusetts Wildlife.

While Dale had to trudge some distance for many of his pictures, he captured inspiring sunrise views taken from the very convenient east-facing Quabbin Overlook behind the New Salem Fire Station. It made me ponder waking up early to view the sunrise there, though that's easier said than done.

After the show, I had an opportunity to visit with several friends who were in the audience, including Peter and Nancy Gerry of Athol. Pete made a very cogent observation—that while the closing of UTD was painful for the town and many residents, it offered a bright and satisfying future to Dale Monette.

Dale has displayed and sold prints at the North Quabbin Garlic and Arts Festival, and Wendell Christmas Crafts Fair. Find information about Dale at his website, northquabbinphotography.com. He can be contacted via the website.

Published in *Athol Daily News*, February 4, 2016
Copyright © 2016 by Newspapers of Massachusetts, Inc.
Used with permission.
Update: Dale has had more wildlife photograph books published and frequently does slide shows to inform and entertain people.

At Ninety-four, Jerry Chiasson Is Still Drumming
2012

Jerry Chaisson, left, and Ethan Stone enjoy cups of coffee.
photo courtesy of Ethan Stone

Jerry Chiasson of Royalston is "ninety-four years young and still swingin' harder than ever," says his musical partner, pianist Ethan Stone of Athol.

A couple of times a month, Stone, 34, drives to Jerry's home, loads up Jerry's drum set, and off they go to a senior living center to bring residents the joy of familiar music of a bygone era.

Stone added, "Jerry's a true hero to me," and he tells how they got together.

> I was playing at a nursing home one afternoon in 2008, and a man was sitting nearby tapping on his chair in time

to the music. I noticed he had great rhythm and asked him if he played drums. He told me he did play drums and his name was Jerry Chiasson. Although Jerry was not in any need of nursing care and at the time was still driving, he was living at the nursing home to be with his wife who required twenty-four-hour care, and he brought her to hear the music programs at the facility.

 I had heard of him before from my father Dick Stone, who performed with Jerry and Mal Hall in various concerts in the 1960s. I suggested that Jerry bring down some drums and sit in with me some time. He did, we had a blast, and we've been playing together ever since.

Ethan is a busy performer and recording artist best known locally as the organizer of Tooltown Live. A 1995 Athol High graduate, Stone graduated from Boston's prestigious Berklee School of Music.

Jerry and Ethan are making a new CD called The Jerry Chiasson Orchestra . . . For the Love of Jazz which will contain some of Jerry's favorite songs arranged for various sized jazz ensembles ranging from the duo up to a big band. Stone and Chiasson are sometimes joined by other musicians, including Richard Chase of Orange on bass guitar.

Jerry started playing the drums when he was fourteen and a student of Ross Hornbeck of Orange. He played for vaudeville acts at the York Theater in Athol, which was part-time work, and also landed a job at the L.S. Starrett Company in the micrometer room.

At nineteen, Jerry joined the US Air Force, worked as a mechanic, and flew on missions with B-24 and B-17 aircraft, but he transferred to special services and started playing in Air Force-sponsored ensembles. Wearing his uniform, he traveled widely, enabling him to meet and play with jazz musicians in fabled New

Orleans and Los Angeles. He met Benny Paine, who played in Cab Calloway's band and was an arranger for blues singer Billy Daniels.

After the war, Chiasson got his old job back at Starrett's and met his soon-to-be-wife Bernice Crumb. The marriage lasted for fifty-six years until Bernice's death in 2008.

He played for many popular local bandleaders including Ken Bartell of Winchendon and Mal Hall of Orange.

I was at the 1794 Meetinghouse in New Salem when jazz vocalist Samirah Evans introduced Jerry, who was in the audience. Jerry, already linked with Ethan Stone, was clearly pleased to be connecting to young musicians. The musicians call themselves "Samirah Evans and her Handsome Devils." One of them was pianist Miro Sprague, then a resident of Erving, whose virtuoso piano playing brought down the house.

Sprague, 27, was planning a move from Massachusetts to Los Angeles to study for a master's degree at the Thelonius Monk Institute of Jazz Performance, building on the bachelor's degree he obtained at the Manhattan School of Music in New York.

Another dedicated young pianist from the area is Adam Bergeron, who plays classical piano for seniors and is busy in the studio creating a new CD. The rock 'n roll band that includes Adam on keyboards, the Lee Villaire Band, is also working on a new CD. As children, Bergeron and longtime friend Stone both studied piano with the Sisters of the Assumption in Petersham.

"Sister Germaine Fournier in Petersham gave me my first piano lessons," Ethan says, "and she was awesome.

She let me play any styles I wanted as long as I put my best effort into them. Of course, this made me want to practice all the time! She had an infectious enthusiasm for music and life, and I caught it."

That enthusiasm is something that apparently works well for these fine musicians, young and old.

Published in Athol Daily News, May 3, 2012
Copyright © 2012 by Newspapers of Massachusetts, Inc.
Used with permission.

Update: Jerry Chaisson died in September 2012. Ethan Stone, while still a musician, is also a businessman selling Christmas trees and firewood.

Meet My New Neighbor, Jesse Rix, a Tattoo Artist

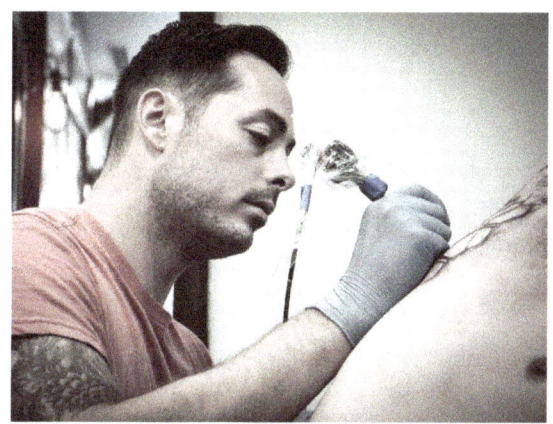

Tattoo artist Jesse Rix works intently.
photo courtesy of Jesse Rix

Jesse Rix of Royalston, who liked art when he was a teenager, also liked tattoos, and even acquired a couple of them before he turned twenty.

Told by some adults he might seek a career as a graphic designer, he rejected that because, he said, "I was not interested." While tattooing started out as a hobby, he calculated early on that it could be a good way to earn a living.

Jesse, who is thirty-one, was only twenty-two when he opened his own business, Secret Lake Tattoo, located in Keene, New Hampshire, as he was residing nearby. It was named after the area in Phillipston where he used to live. He bought the equipment that is used for putting ink into skin and taught himself how to use it. A tattoo on his arm—a sleeve in the parlance of the industry—features a guitar with wings. He did it to himself.

A more recent sleeve, a colorful floral pattern on the arm of Jesse's wife, Danielle, is also his creation. Jesse, who graduated from Athol High School in 2001, is the son of Harry and Denise Rix of Phillipston. Danielle, Mahar Regional School Class of 2003, is the daughter of Kim and Craig Parker, now divorced, formerly of Orange. Jesse and Danielle have a seven-month-old son named Levi who stared at me with big bright eyes when I visited them in their nearby home.

Danielle and Jesse Rix
photo courtesy of Jesse Rix

Jesse's studio is at 196 Main Street, Keene. When he closed Secret Lake Tattoo, Jesse wrote on the website, "I look forward to the opportunities that owning the private studio will offer and to be able to focus more attention to my customers, tattoos, and artwork." Go to his new website, jesserixtattoos.com, to see Jesse's outstanding portfolio. His designs are in a very realistic style, and he often favors black and gray inks, though hundreds of colors are now available.

The machines to apply tattoos originally used electric coil technology, something like a doorbell, but Jesse has acquired a high-speed, up-to-date rotary system. Needles and ink caps are disposable, and artists are trained to maintain high standards of hygiene.

Jesse works with his clients to come up with a final design. He talks to each individual about his or her reason for wanting a tattoo and takes skin type into consideration. Tattoos often memorialize an individual or a milestone for the recipient and sometimes "it's just for the love of the art," he told me. He informs clients that tattoos can require extra attention in the future to maintain color intensity.

Jesse also reminds clients that "it's forever," though doctors and nurse practitioners using lasers can remove tattoos. Jesse won't do racist or Satanic designs, and he obeys regulations in New Hampshire that require a person getting a tattoo to be at least eighteen years old. According to Jesse, most of his clients are between twenty-one and fifty.

Since that is about the age range of the four women and three men who work full-time in the newsroom of the *Athol Daily News*, I decided to survey them about tattoos. Two out of the seven already have tattoos. One of them has four and wants more, but "the only thing stopping me is money." Two who do not have tattoos have been considering it.

Reporter Jared Robinson emailed me:

> I don't have a tattoo. That doesn't mean I haven't thought about it frequently. My wife and I considered getting some kind of matching tattoos after our trip to Hawaii last year to commemorate the trip but couldn't decide on what to get. Every time I get close to the point of getting a tattoo I get hung up on the whole "this thing is permanent" notion, and I can't think of anything to get that I could be happy with for such a long haul.
>
> Jesse was at AHS for much of the same time I was. And his sister was in many of the same classes as me, so if I were to get a tattoo, he would be my first choice to do the work.

Jesse doesn't have to worry about customers as he seems to have quite a reputation. According to his website, he is booked through August. His rate is $150 an hour, with an average tattoo taking four to six hours (that is, $600 to $750). He added, "Full sleeves and back pieces can take a long time, involving multiple sessions. I've had some sleeves take as long as 60 hours spread out over a year." He noted that the average hourly rate in the region is about $100, with artists in urban centers such as Los Angeles and New York charging $200 an hour.

Does getting tattooed hurt? "Yup," said Jesse, but he explained that after a while, the recipient's endorphins—natural pain suppressors—kick in, plus Jesse has some techniques to help people bear the discomfort. I asked Jesse if he has any interest in piercings, and he said, "No, but people can do what they want."

Tattooing is "one of the boom industries in this country," he said, and it's also big overseas. Last October, Jesse traveled to Evian, France, for a convention attended by thousands of people, with two hundred artists setting up booths. He has attended conventions in Colorado, too, where there is "more about art," with a focus on collegiality and on media other than ink and skin.

Jesse clearly enjoys what he is doing and maintains high standards in a field that some people might disdain. He is aware of the fact that despite its popularity nowadays, tattooing remains somewhat taboo, associated in popular culture for decades with drunken sailors and assorted bad guys. *Wikipedia* offers detailed entries for "tattoo" and "process of tattooing."

Times have certainly changed and, as Jesse puts it, "It's nice to make a living doing something that you love, that you're passionate about."

Do I have a tattoo? No, but I respect freedom of choice in such matters.

Published in *Athol Daily News,* March 27, 2014
Copyright © 2014 by Newspapers of Massachusetts, Inc.
Used with permission.

Love, Adventure, Community Define a Couple's Life
2010

Ruth Suyenaga and Mark Shoul
photo courtesy of Mark Shoul

Ruth Suyenaga and Mark Shoul, friends of mine for more than twenty-five years, invited me to separate community events this month, and I'm extending these invitations today to readers of this column while also telling you a little about the dynamic married couple.

The event that Ruth invited me to was an art show called Teachers as Artists, featuring her lush watercolor prints as well as the work of several colleagues who teach art in Gardner public schools. The exhibition took place in the East Wing Gallery of Mount Wachusett Community College.

I attended a reception and was impressed at the talent of the dedicated teachers, including another North Quabbin resident, Frances LeMieux of Phillipston.

Mark's event was open to everyone who lives in the North Quabbin region, as the organization he leads, called Hands Across North Quabbin or HANDS, launched an ambitious campaign to promote community collaboration.

Sponsored by HANDS and its five campaign partners including Athol-Royalston and Mahar regional school districts, Orange Ministerial Association, Athol Lions Club, and Athol Area YMCA, the event was a large-scale potluck BBQ dinner. It took place under the new community pavilion at Silver Lake Park in Athol with the large grille fired up and HANDS providing dessert and beverages. Mark promised me a hot dog, and I brought fresh greens from my garden to share.

The goal of the campaign was to create a civic culture based on collaboration and overcoming differences by finding ways to work cooperatively toward progress rather than getting bogged down in conflict. Mark said that

> civic culture consists of the core values and beliefs that drive how people in a community, state, or nation think about and act toward each other around the need to solve common problems or create shared opportunities.

Mark and I, though not native to the area, both have acquired great affection for the North Quabbin region and seek, each in his own way, to celebrate, strengthen, and protect the unique community we have found here.

As a couple, Mark and Ruth come from very different places and yet have shared values that keep them together and enable them to support one another while contributing significantly to the community.

Love, adventure, and community define their lives. While their personalities are different, they have a quality that makes me want to be their friend—the ability to be both serious and fun-loving.

Ruth, of Japanese ancestry, was born and raised in Hawaii. Mark, of Eastern European Jewish ancestry, was born and raised in the Boston suburb of Newton. Each of them started out with great affection for family and heritage, an affection that continues. While valuing their roots, however, they became lovers and life partners seeking something new and fresh as they faced the future. They met as students of anthropology at New York University, and upon leaving college in the early 1970s, the couple went on an adventure to South America, living in very rustic conditions in an isolated village on the Pacific coast of Colombia.

When they finally settled on land in Royalston, they set out to raise a family and put down new roots in this community. Their two children, Maile, 30, and Kenji, 22, attended local public schools and are now pursuing their own dreams.

Ruth became an art teacher, working for eight years in Royalston and seventeen years in Gardner, with as many as two hundred students. She has a special interest in helping parents understand the value of nurturing creativity in children.

Mark's first venture in community organizing hereabouts was the creation of a barter network which, by the way, helped me get a free easy chair which is still in my living room. He then focused for a time on affordable housing and was instrumental in completing successful projects on Oxbow Road in Orange and Liberty

Lane in Royalston. More recently, he founded an organization called the Institute for Community Building which has evolved into Hands Across North Quabbin.

Published in *Athol Daily News,* June 10, 2010
Copyright © 2010 by Newspapers of Massachusetts, Inc.
Used with permission.

Update: Mark and Ruth are both retired and spend as much time as they can with family and friends. They have been active in South Royalston revitalization efforts.

Kathy Morris, Scientist/Librarian, Wheat Weaver
2017

Kathy Morris
photo courtesy of Kathy Morris

Kathy Morris of Royalston, after being fully committed to a career in highly specialized advanced science, has developed an interest in two distinct aspects of fiber arts and crafts—the historic palm leaf hat industry and her own creation of artistic wheat weavings.

I never heard of wheat weavings until I saw Kathy doing them. I admired their intricacy and the fact that they were so unusual—and that they used a plant that is so basic to the human diet. Eating wheat, usually ground into flour for baking bread or making pasta, is so common, but seeing it assembled to make something beautiful and decorative was a pleasant surprise.

Before sitting down to write my column, I took a close look at the wheat weaving hanging between two windows in my kitchen, and I focused on its intricacy and counted a total of twenty-five wheat stalks with their grain heads braided together in a unique creation. I purchased my wheat weaving when Kathy had a booth at the North Quabbin Garlic & Arts Festival. She sells her creations at the Amherst Farmers' Market.

Kathy is director of the Phinehas S. Newton Library in Royalston and is married to organic farmer Larry Siegel, with whom she maintains a rustic rural life on a scenic gravel road. The couple came to Royalston in the late 1970s to have a homestead and raise their family. The late Martha Kirkman, justice of the peace, performed their nuptials on New Year's Eve, December 31, 1977.

At that time, Kathy was still working as a scientist based on undergraduate and graduate education at Michigan State University. Her doctorate is in microbiology and her post-doctoral work in cellular immunology. What brought her to Massachusetts was employment in her field at research laboratories affiliated with Harvard Medical School. She commuted from Royalston to the city for seven and one-half years.

As she started a family, she continued to work but soon left her career behind. Larry went to work as a cook at the Common Ground, a natural foods restaurant in Brattleboro, Vermont, and the couple homeschooled the boys. By now, Benjamin, 39; Jacob, 37; Noah, 35; and Joshua, 32, have all found their own unique ways in the world, and I could readily write an "Inside/Outside" column about each one of them. Actually, I already did—about Noah, the mushroom specialist!

Kathy became a self-taught weaver after an experience at Canterbury, New Hampshire, Shaker Village. She recounted, "I saw a woman who was weaving wheat there, and she told me she learned from a book, so I came back and ordered every book I could find through inter-library loan. "Larry had been growing wheat for baby food, part of the family's almost one hundred percent homegrown diet, and the grain was also grown for use in dried flower arrangements that they sold.

Kathy continued, "A couple of years after that, the Friends of the Library wanted me to do a program and I didn't have enough wheat, so I went online and discovered suppliers of wheat stalks and the National Association of Wheat Weavers NAWW, nawwstraw.org.

She attended her first NAWW convention in 2006 in Albuquerque and returned in 2017 from the gathering in Indianapolis. Kathy enjoys learning more from experienced wheat weavers and she, in turn, has given classes in our region. One of her successful students is Molly Divoll of Royalston.

By coincidence, the man for whom the Royalston library is named, Phinehas S. Newton, made his fortune in the fiber arts industry—the weaving of palm leaf hats in the late 1800s. Newton gave the town ten thousand dollars for construction of the brick and sandstone building that graces the north end of the town common and bears a cornerstone dated 1910.

Somewhere between an industry and a craft, the palm leaf hat business is an important if small chapter in the history of Massachusetts and especially this region. Newton's wealth came from the system known as "putting out." The raw palm leaf material came from Cuba, and after being cleaned, bleached, and split, it was ready for weaving. Included was an aesthetic aspect because of the wide variety of decorative braids or plaits used to make hats.

Phinehas's brother Charles Newton owned a store, and he was part of the barter—no cash—system. The raw material was taken into people's homes, and over the winter, women wove hats, delivering them to the store where they got credit they could spend down for necessities. Researching the topic, Kathy learned that in 1853, there were five stores in Royalston involved in the industry.

A Harvard Forest history of Petersham includes this: "A normal winter's work was 250 hats, for which they were paid at the rate of ten cents each. In 1836, 130,525 hats were made in Petersham." Kathy informed me that in 1837 there were two million hats made in Worcester County alone, involving thousands of workers. It became a large industry—for example, $3.3 million worth of hats statewide in 1860. Kathy found no record of the number of hats made in Royalston.

Times have changed, but up until the mid-twentieth century, almost everyone, male and female, wore hats! I remember in the 1950s visiting Macy's department store in New York City, going up in an elevator, and hearing the operator announce the millinery—or hat—department. I don't think any store has a millinery department these days!

Kathy was the featured speaker at a fund-raising dinner for the Royalston Historical Society that needed money for a new roof on its building. We all enjoyed a dinner cooked by townspeople and gave Kathy a big round of applause after her informative presentation on both palm leaf hats and wheat weaving.

Published in *Athol Daily News*, May 11, 2017
Copyright © 2017 by Newspapers of Massachusetts, Inc.
Used with permission.

Maureen Blasco, Unsung Hero of Royalston
2018

In a recent issue of the Royalston Community Newsletter, editor Beth Gospodarek invited readers to submit the names of local residents who are unsung heroes. She started by suggesting two individuals—assessor Jim Richardson and community activist Maureen Blasco.

Beth herself was deservedly honored as an unsung heroine in 2008 by the Massachusetts Commission on the Status of Women, and it seems appropriate for one community dynamo to want to give credit to others.

Maureen Blasco in her garden
photo by Ruth Suyenaga

I hope to write about Jim another day, but this column is devoted to Maureen, and from what I have learned about her, there isn't enough space for me to tell the whole story. "Community activist," the phrase I used in the opening paragraph, is hardly adequate. Maureen, a modest person, was not keen on the idea that I would write about her, but I insisted.

Recently, several women friends, almost all of them from Royalston, gathered to celebrate Maureen's sixty-fifth birthday. When I asked those friends to tell me about Maureen, they listed many accomplishments and activities but stressed their affection for her as a valued, trusted friend.

Her generosity was frequently mentioned, including the fact she offers lodging at her home on Norcross Road to those in need—people, dogs, horses.

Beth noted that Maureen "always fights for justice," Librarian Kathy Morris noted she is "always there behind the scenes," and Norah Dooley called her "the most loyal and stalwart friend in the world."

Ruth described her as having an "emerald thumb," adding,

> Long ago, she was one of gardening staff for the Public Broadcasting System Victory Garden show and has a huge truck garden from which she preserves and processes organic vegetables and fruit that take her through the winter.

Maureen has been in this region for thirty-two years, starting with several years at Bittersweet Farm in Winchendon, which pioneered community supported agriculture, CSA. She moved to Royalston in 1998 and continued to focus on growing food for herself and others.

She was born in Passaic, New Jersey, near New York City, went to Roman Catholic grade school in Passaic and Clifton, New Jersey, High School. She lived in Connecticut and Michigan before coming to Massachusetts.

Her education included Ohio State University and Boston University, followed by degrees from Wheelock College, Boston, and UMass, Amherst.

With a strong devotion to public education, Maureen commented, "I care very much about giving children the kinds of experiences they need to grow, mature, and understand the world in its complexity."

She retired recently from teaching. Her career included working in a group home for emotionally disturbed urban children and running an afterschool program in Fitchburg. She obtained a public-school job in Winchendon, where she mainly taught kindergarten for twenty-seven years. She has also been an active member of the Athol-Royalston Education Foundation, AREF, which raises money to provide enrichment programs for public schools in the two towns. In post-retirement gigs, she has taught preschool and English as a second language in the Athol-Royalston district.

Love of nature has brought Maureen to rural Massachusetts, the same path that many of my friends and I have followed. She explained,

> Currently, of course, I'm working against the pipeline. But for me, it is an issue of energy policy, climate change, and the pollution of the air, land, and sea. These things make me feel compelled to try to influence the future of our energy sources—from fossil fuels to renewables and efficiency and changing our lifestyles. Working with neighbors this year has proven to us all that we can effect change.

Maureen's work with the Friends of the Phinehas Newton Library includes helping librarian Kathy Morris, Patti Stanko, and others host special events and getting the monthly newsletter in the mail plus assisting with a spring plant sale and summertime Shakespeare production featuring local children.

She is a member of the Ladies Benevolent Society and the Royalston Conservation Commission.

Another activity Maureen enjoys is horseback riding with Beth Gospodarek and Robert Fairchild of Royalston as longtime riding partners.

Maureen is also an artist. Norah Dooley noted,

> Maybe you have seen how, from creating baked goods to braiding onions from her garden, Maureen infuses beauty into everyday life. She is an accomplished stained-glass artist. She gifted our family with one of her pieces, and every time I look out my kitchen window through the stained-glass flowers, I see a tangible reminder of how, when you are lucky enough to have Maureen as your friend, her kindness is real, beautiful, and enduring.

Her son, Eric Blasco, 29, imbued with a strong interest in sustainability and social justice, works as an urban gardener in Philadelphia. Eric's father is former Athol resident Rudy Perkins.

Summing up Maureen's role, Kathy Morris said, "Loyalty to her friends and family and to her community are the basis of her being."

Considering those values, her behind-the-scenes activity, and authentic modesty, "unsung hero" is the perfect label for Maureen Blasco.

Published in *Athol Daily News*, Feb. 5, 2018
Copyright © 2018 by Newspapers of Massachusetts, Inc.
Used with permission.

At Eighty-seven, Jack Borden Continues to Look at the Sky
2015

"What are those clouds called?" I asked, glancing out from the windows of McDonald's Restaurant on Brookside Road in Athol. The question was directed to Jack Borden, who can be found most mornings with his computer and some reading material in the restaurant's southwest corner booth.

"Stratus," he replied, "but don't be too concerned about the name. Just look."

Appreciation of the sky, including its varied cloud formations, has been Jack's focus for decades. After many years as a popular WBZ-TV, Boston, news reporter and anchor, he founded an educational nonprofit organization called For Spacious Skies.

Jack, who recently turned eighty-seven and lives with his wife, Jan, in a condominium on Brickyard Road in Athol, became intensely involved with sky awareness soon after an "epiphany," as he calls it, that took place in the Wachusett Meadow Sanctuary of Massachusetts Audubon Society in Princeton. He and Jan were lying down on the grass, and, as he recalls, "suddenly the sky became a huge dome with a never-ending show of sound, light, and movement."

He soon made two other discoveries. First, most people went about their lives with a total lack of awareness of the sky above them, and second, that by focusing on the sky and increasing their awareness of it, people of all ages could measurably improve their lives.

Looking up was relaxing and fun, Jack knew. The focus of For Spacious Skies has always been educational, based on use of mass media to sustain public awareness. Jack proved effective at winning the attention of print and television journalists. An article in the April 1994 *Smithsonian* magazine was headlined, "Up in the sky, there's a good time to be had everywhere, always for free." A Harvard study provided proof of the value of skywatching for students' success in their intellectual development.

For Spacious Skies soon obtained support from businesses and foundations which enabled Jack and his colleagues to develop educational programs that impacted schoolchildren as well as senior citizens. Scientists, educators, artists, and people from many walks of life became involved with For Spacious Skies. Among those who served on the organization's board of directors was the famed photographer Ansel Adams, who had become alarmed at declining air quality and its impact on the way the sky was viewed.

Jack was born in Hartford and feels a strong connection to his secular Jewish heritage which nurtured his quest for knowledge as well as his sense of humor. He is a proud graduate of Hartford's Weaver High School, Class of 1945. He joined the US Army in 1946, serving eighteen months, including time in Japan. After his discharge, he benefited from the GI Bill—financial aid for veterans—to study at the University of Vermont, University of Missouri Journalism School, and University of Connecticut, where he obtained a bachelor's degree.

His first media job was as a radio disc jockey, but he soon became a television news reporter, finding a home at WBZ-TV, Channel 4, a leading news source in the Boston area sometimes called "the big socket" in homage to its then owner, Westinghouse Electric Corporation.

Jack loved the variety that comes with news reporting. He was "interested in everything" and liked being "out in the street meeting people." Sometimes Jan accompanied him, as when they came to this area to do a piece about the growing fascination with spiritualist Elwood Babbit, who resided on a small farm in Northfield near the Warwick town line.

The couple sought outdoor activities, sometimes with the Appalachian Mountain Club, taking them from their suburban home in Lexington to central and western Massachusetts. They came to Orange in the 1960s for the international skydiving tournament, and Jan (but not Jack) decided to take a couple of jumps herself.

In the 1970s, Jack got a part-time job teaching at Mount Wachusett Community College in Gardner. He became popular and was the Mount's commencement speaker one year. The job in Gardner provided frequent opportunity to drive around the area, and Jack remembers dining at Bellinger's in downtown Athol.

One time, they happened to meet Richard "Obie" O'Brien of New Salem, a Metropolitan District Commission, MDC, police officer whose duties sometimes included Quabbin Reservoir patrols. Jan got the idea of opening a bakery in a vacant former gas station that Obie owned. Her vision eventually became Yankee Strudel, an outstanding gourmet pastry bakery that she owned and operated for ten years.

The couple moved to the Brickyard Road condo development in 1989. Jack had departed a few years earlier from WBZ and worked in various positions, including a substitute reporter at WCVB-TV, Boston's Channel 5, and Cable News Network, CNN.

For Spacious Skies eventually became a full-time occupation, and Jack found it ironic that his strong interest in variety shifted to such a specific focus—"a one-act pony, the sky," he said jokingly.

For Spacious Skies had a beautiful cloud chart endorsed by the National Weather Service and Weather Channel.

Published in *Athol Daily News,* April 23, 2015
Copyright © 2015 by Newspapers of Massachusetts, Inc.
Used with permission.
Update: Jack Bordon died in 2020
two years after the death of his wife, Jan.

Paul McGinnis: A Lifetime as Logger, Teamster, and Sawyer
2013

"Allen, if you push the right memory buttons, he has some great stories to tell, things that happened before cherry-picking logging trucks and the dawn of the chain saw and the skidder. Plus he is just plain fun to listen to."

I followed through on that suggestion from my friend Ronnie DeJackome of Petersham and sat down to talk with Paul McGinnis of New Salem, who spent most of his life dealing with trees—chopping them down, loading them on a logging sled, hauling it with a team of horses, and sawing them up into lumber.

Now eighty-two, McGinnis lives with his wife, the former Eleanor Mealand, in a historic home on Old County Road, the very house in which he was born.

McGinnis' life story reflects hard work—including narrow escape from danger—as well as tragedy and adventure.

The tragedy took place in 1941 when he was only eleven and saw his father drown in Petersham's Harvard Pond, then called Brooks Pond. As with many area ponds, trees felled during the Hurricane of 1938 were being stored for eventual processing. That day, young Paul was helping his dad, Leo McGinnis, and his uncle Wayne McGinnis use ropes and booms to bring the logs to the shore for cutting up on a portable sawmill.

None of the trio could swim, and when Leo McGinnis's foot went through the bottom of a boat they were using, he ended up slipping between the logs and perishing in the water.

Paul's friendship and collaboration with his Uncle Wayne continued for decades. Both competed in several country fairs, with Wayne specializing in oxen pulls and Paul using horses. They both won many awards.

Paul's oldest grandchild, Leo Lacaswan, who works as a skidder operator, is honored with the name of Paul's father and continues the family forestry tradition. Paul and young Leo have teamed up to win crosscut sawing contests, pulling huge blades back and forth just the way that a pair of men felled trees before the use of chain saws. Skidders are machines with huge tires that have replaced teams of horses in the woods.

Horses play a role in two of Paul's more exciting stories. In one incident in the early 1950s, he was transporting four horses on a truck on Route 5 in Connecticut, just south of Springfield, when a car cut him off at an intersection. The truck was smashed, the man in the car died, and Paul was trapped in the truck for nearly an hour, but the horses survived without serious injury because of the way they were protected by harnesses and blankets.

On another occasion, while logging in woods on a steep hill in Ashfield, a runner chain—a sort of braking device on a logging sled—broke and created a dangerous situation. Paul said, "I hollered at the bay horse, and it turned a corner," thus saving the whole rig from crashing into trees.

Paul loved working with horses, primarily the Percheron and Belgian breeds, and felt a great compatibility with them. "I wouldn't even have to pick up the reins, just speak to them," he said.

Portable sawmills were frequently used so that trees could be downed and cut up on site. The men moved the sawmill from site to site, taking along portable shacks that became a home away from home for weeks, even months. While logging or sawing, Paul sometimes hit blade-destroying obstacles such as horseshoes, insulators, barbed wire, nails, and bolts, even a 50-caliber bullet from a cannon that workers from the L S Starrett Company had made to shoot for fun at the Athol Rod and Gun Club. He was a sawyer at Bill Robinson's sawmill in the Wheelwright section of Hardwick from 1967 until retirement in 1994. In recent years, McGinnis has been somewhat slowed by health problems, but he still has his heart in the woods and an affection for the array of old hand tools as well as some modern machinery stored in his barn and a shed.

The McGinnis home, near Quabbin Gate 35, was the scene of some heartbreaking times in the late 1930s, indelible childhood memories, when friends and neighbors stopped by for a final farewell as the creation of the Quabbin Reservoir forced their relocation.

Paul and Eleanor McGinnis have four daughters and eight grandchildren. The adventure in Paul's life included lots of travel with his wife covering every state except Hawaii. Paul was active in New Salem's civic life, including thirty years as assessor and service on the planning board as well as the fire department. A photograph of the couple graces the cover of the 2004 town report.

Published in *Athol Daily News*, Feb. 14, 2013
Copyright © 2013 by Newspapers of Massachusetts, Inc.
Used with permission.
Update: Paul McGinnis died in 2018,
and his wife, Eleanor, died in 2022.

Betty Kimball of Orange Is Really Good at Restoring Old Homes

2017

Betty Kimball
photo by Faye Vollinger

Decades ago, David Belcher, reporter for the Orange Enterprise and Journal, penned an article entitled "Some People Love to Restore Old Homes."

That article featured Orange resident Betty Kimball, now eighty-three, who continues to do what she loves. Despite her age, Betty not only plans and designs but also does most of the physical work related to her projects.

Physical work includes painting and scraping, glazing plank-frame windows using antique wavy glass, climbing a ladder to nail down hand-split wooden shakes on a roof, and carrying gravel in a wheelbarrow for driveway maintenance.

With silver-white pigtails on either side of her face and sometimes referring to her "boyfriend" John Kaltner (former owner of Super John's grocery store in Greenfield), Betty exudes the same youthful enthusiasm I observed in her when we first met in the 1970s.

At that time, she was working restoring her North Orange home that she calls The Tavern. The dark-brown Colonial-era building was sold a few years ago to a woman from Texas.

The Tavern, purchased with Betty's late husband Curtis Kimball, proprietor of Kimball-Cooke Insurance, is where Betty and Curt raised their two children, Dan and Curtis. The older Curtis, who initially introduced Betty to New England antiques and the concept of old-house restoration, died in 2001, two years after the younger Curtis (only thirty-nine) died of cancer. Betty considered The Tavern to be one of Orange's most important historic buildings, and though the family "lived in the mess" for a long time, the building's restoration is a well-earned pride and joy.

The Tavern was not the Kimballs' first home in Orange. That was the Indian Mound House on Briggs Street.

Betty's son Dan, a Phillipston and Petersham police officer, now married and father of two, lives in North Orange, in a house across Main Street from The Tavern. Betty is a frequent visitor to her son's home, visiting grandchildren Max and Erin, nicknamed Rosebud.

Betty is the eldest of the Hall girls, the six daughters of Mal and Pearl Hall of Orange. She lived in New Salem before moving back to Orange, and she has a home on Old Hickory Road, Lake Mattawa. While chatting in her living room there, Betty showed me some old newspaper and magazine clippings. In one of them, she was a teen-ager modeling a bathing suit as one of the Jantzen girls when the brand Jantzen marked classy women's bathing suits.

Two of her houses, the Tavern and one on Athol Road in North Orange that she calls The Little Brown House, were featured in the prestigious Early American Life magazine. She lived in the Little Brown House for five years after selling The Tavern.

Her father was known as Mister Music, and it's no surprise that Betty played flute and saxophone when she was young and sang on stage, too. Betty recalls her initial fascination with an antique Cape Cod-style house when, as a child, she visited a pair of elderly sisters, Sadie and Jake, who resided together on Quarry Road in Warwick. Referring to the house, not the sisters, Betty commented, "I always loved the old."

Betty is very enthusiastic about her most recent project, Charlotte's Cottage, moved from Daniel Shays Highway in Orange to its current location on Holtshire Road. It is named for one of the Hall girls, who is deceased. The building has been lovingly restored in recent years but would probably not serve as a home for a modern family because it is exceedingly and authentically rustic.

Located nearby on the other side of Holtshire Road is one of her completed projects, now the home of Tim and Wendy Cornwell.

One of Betty's houses with the date 1771 painted on the chimney is suitable for modern living. It is what she calls her Village House at 180 Athol Road, North Orange. It is for sale, listed with Tina Kolb Diaz, a Realtor from Cambridge who purchased the Little Brown House from Betty a few years ago.

When not fixing up old houses, picking blueberries, or hanging out with John or her grandchildren, Betty enjoys traditional rug braiding — she has dozens of such works of art in her various houses. As part of her strong-willed commitment to staying active and youthful, she also walks almost daily from the Lake House to Charlotte's Cottage, two miles each way. It fits perfectly with a sign in the window of the Village House that says Act Old Later.

Published in *Athol Daily News,* July 6, 2017
Copyright © 2017 by Newspapers of Massachusetts, Inc.
Used with permission.

Update: Signficant loss of eyesight has slowed Betty down, but her zest for life and love of old houses continues.

*Local Women on Motorcycles Travel
to Motor Maids' Gathering
2014*

Johanna Lawlor-Moore, left, and Darlene Lawlor-Moore
photo courtesy of Johanna Lawlor-Moore

Retired Massachusetts State Police Sergeant Johanna Lawlor-Moore of Athol projected photographs on the wall of the Millers River Environmental Center to present an informative, humorous, and sometimes harrowing narrative about her past summer's adventure.

The guest speaker at a recent meeting of the North Quabbin Trails Association, NQTA, of which she is a member, she recounted how she and her spouse, Darlene Lawlor-Moore, departed from Athol in June of 2013, heading for Bend, Oregon, for the Seventy-Third Annual Conference of the Motor Maids, a national women's motorcycle organization founded in 1940.

The duo joined forces with motorcycle riders Mary Robinson and Nancy Watkins of Connecticut on the five-week journey that included a lot of sightseeing and exciting riding, most of it on two-lane paved roads, many without guardrails. Johanna noted, "The curvier the roads, the better."

Johanna is the district director of Motor Maids for Massachusetts, Rhode Island, and Connecticut. Her talk at the Millers River Environmental Center, where NQTA members gather monthly, included images and information about the unusual group founded by Linda Dugeau of Providence, Rhode Island. The history lesson included a photograph of Bessie Springfield, 1911–1993, the first African-American woman to ride solo across the United States.

About 350 women from Canada and the US came together in Oregon— all arriving on motorcycles and all conforming to the membership requirement that women in Motor Maids legally own and operate their own bike or one belonging to a family member.

Johanna made the journey on her 2009 BMW F650GS with Darlene on a 2001 Harley-Davidson

Electra Glide. Nancy rode a Kawasaki Drifter and Mary a Kawasaki Mean Streak.

Johanna began her talk by pointing out that over time she had undertaken a wide variety of out-of-door activities including hiking, mountaineering, kayaking, bicycling, tennis, golf, SCUBA diving, piloting an airplane, ice-climbing, snowboarding, snowshoeing, and more, but that the trip to Oregon was one of her more rigorous motorcycle journeys.

A significant motorcycle trip such as that one, she said, like any similar activity with several people involved, requires attention to such issues as weather, equipment, level of ability, and speed. The trip involved months of careful planning. Johanna pointed out that on her motorcycle she carried clothing, rain gear, maps, camping equipment, tools, and a cooler (sometimes used for adult beverages to be consumed only at the end of the day's travel), and more.

The women endured rainstorms, near-freezing weather in the Rocky Mountains, and temperatures of more than a hundred degrees in areas such as the Badlands of South Dakota. The places they stayed camping and in a few hotels included "some nice places and some not so nice," Johanna commented. Unusual signs amused the women, for example "Snowmobiles must yield to aircraft at all times," and "Eat here or we both starve."

One of the first places visited as they headed west was the Women's Rights National Historic Park in Seneca Falls, New York. The most famous national parks they traversed were Yellowstone and Grand Tetons. But there were also less known sites such as Crater Lake National Park, Wind Cave National Park, Pompey's Pillar National Monument, John Day

Fossil Beds National Monument, Pipestone National Monument, and some state parks.

Johanna was especially intrigued by the strange landscape of the Toadstool Geologic Park in the Oglala National Grassland of Nebraska.

They rode a sixty-nine-mile section of US Highway 212 in Montana and Wyoming known as Beartooth Highway and officially designated as a National Scenic Byway All-American Road. They saw snow-capped mountains including the Sawtooth Range near Stanley, Idaho; visited Cooke City General Store in a Montana town where mining once flourished; and were awed by the enormous redwood trees along the northern California coastline.

Accidents do happen, alas, and a sudden hairpin turn on California Highway 1 north of Fort Bragg, California, caused Darlene's bike to crash, and she ended up in a local hospital for several days being treated for broken ribs and a collapsed lung. As Johanna put it, "When the world throws mud at you, you make mud pies," so while Nancy and Mary continued to ride their bikes, Johanna and Darlene had theirs shipped home and rented a car so that Darlene could continue to heal and travel in comfort and safety for the return trip to Athol.

Averaging 250-450 miles a day, their motorcycle and automobile odyssey lasted about five weeks.

Johanna and Darlene are not giving up on adventure and have more trips planned for 2014, including a trek in Provence, France, and motorcycle rides in Texas and Ireland.

Published in *Athol Daily News*, January 23, 2014

Copyright © 2014 by Newspapers of Massachusetts, Inc.

Used with permission.

Dynamic Well-Known Athol Couple Leaving for Arizona
2018

Jeff Plotkin, Allen Young, and Deb Plotkin, from left
photo by Diane Keijzer

There is a North Quabbin region love story that started on a summer day in 1980 around 6 a.m. in Athol at the intersection of Elizabeth Street and South Athol Road when two joggers almost collided.

In just a few days, a new chapter in their story will begin when Deborah and Jeff Plotkin, a dynamic couple who grew strong roots in the North Quabbin, get in their car and head for a new home in Prescott, Arizona

On that morning thirty-eight years ago, Deb was running into South Athol Road from Elizabeth Street where she almost ran into Jeff Plotkin. Fitness, not romance, was on the minds of both of them that morning. Deb, the mother of a toddler named Derrick, was on the verge of divorce. She was definitely not thinking about men and was startled to encounter one.

Jeff, one of Athol's most eligible bachelors, took immediate notice of that "beautiful woman" (his words) and, as Deb put it, "He didn't stop talking."

She didn't even give him her name. Within seconds, they went their separate ways.

Not too long afterward, however, they had their first date. Deb, who had purchased an item from Jeff's uncle, Sherman Plotkin, at the Plotkin Furniture Store on Exchange Street, returned there on business. Jeff, working the sales floor, saw her and started a conversation that led to a movie date —and then to more dates.

Deb was willing to take a new man into her life who'd be a good father to Derrick, and soon she perceived that Jeff would qualify. Jeff had strong preferences for a Jewish girl, and Deb, nominally Episcopalian but not active in a church, readily converted with the help of a friendly rabbi in Leominster.

Two years after the jogging encounter, with the support of Deb's parents Brian and Barbara Sweatman (both deceased), and Jeff's parents Charlie and Natalie Plotkin (both in their 90s and living in Florida), the happy couple was married in Athol's Temple Israel. As a longtime friend of the Plotkin family, I attended the joyous wedding. The couple lived together briefly on Sanders Street and then purchased a home on the shore of Sportsman's Pond, both in Athol. Jeff adopted Derrick, who took the Plotkin name as Charlie and Natalie embraced him as their grandchild.

Eventually, Jeff decided to retire and closed down Plotkin Furniture, (which he had taken over from his father and uncle). Shortly afterwards, Deb, nearing retirement age from a long career as a family nurse practitioner, had many long talks with Jeff, and together they made plans to sell their Athol home and move to Arizona.

Since the sale of the Pinedale Road lake house on Sportsman's, they've lived temporarily in a rented cottage in Petersham, filled with boxes of possessions. Professional movers will load the boxes up and head west, and a few days after that, the couple will hit the road in their car, destination Prescott, where a contractor has just completed their new house.

As a business owner, Jeff always contributed to community activities. He returned to Athol to run the store after having lived for a year on a kibbutz in Israel, where he felt he had "a patriotic duty to help the Jewish homeland. "Prior to that, Jeff obtained a liberal arts education, garnering a bachelor's degree from the American College in Arundel, Sussex, England. He'd begun his studies at Syracuse University in New York State and also attended New England College in Henniker, New Hampshire.

Deb started out as a licensed practical nurse, then became a registered nurse, adding on a bachelor's degree at Fitchburg State and a master's from the University of Massachusetts, Worcester. She briefly was director of nursing at Applewood nursing home in Winchester, New Hampshire, then became nurse-manager at Athol Memorial Hospital's Community Health Service. She and I were colleagues at AMH when I was vice president of community relations and she was vice president of patient care.

After the AMH management shift in 1999, Deb continued to expand her horizon, studying at UMass, Amherst, to become a licensed nurse practitioner. She was a primary care clinician for several years at North Quabbin Family Physicians, and in recent years at Heywood Medical Group's Tully Family Medicine. Home life was important to Deb and Jeff, who had two more children—Joshua, 34, and Danielle Kya, 31. Josh moved to California and became an advanced yoga instructor. Kya is an emergency room nurse in Charleston, South Carolina. Derrick, 41, who works as a site manager for a major construction company, is married and father of a toddler.

With part of the family out west and motivated by a desire to leave harsh winters behind, Jeff and Deb did lots of research and chose Prescott, Arizona, a city of forty-five thousand that has cultural amenities and some of the look and feel of New England.

Raising their three children in Athol in a home that welcomed dozens of adults and youngsters to many social gatherings small and large was an essential part of community life for Deb and Jeff. Temple Israel also provided valuable camaraderie. A farewell party for the couple took place there.

Both Jeff and Deb speak with enthusiasm about how this community offered them secure, enjoyable lives and how they reciprocated. During heart-to-heart talks, the couple weighed the pros and cons of relocating. They summed up their decision by stating, "It's our time now."

Published in *Athol Daily News,* May 10, 2018
Copyright © 2018 by Newspapers of Massachusetts, Inc.
Used with permission.

Chris Donelan: A Progressive Sheriff Begins His Work
2011

Christopher Donelan
photo courtesy of Christopher Donelan

The old and the new are both dramatically present when a visitor enters the driveway of the Franklin County Jail, 160 Elm Street, Greenfield.

The old (1888) red brick building with its Gothic style architecture stands like a relic alongside the new (2007) gray concrete and stone structure—a modern up-to-date facility.

Christopher Donelan of Orange, elected sheriff to succeed eighteen-year veteran Fred McDonald, is bringing new ideas and a fresh outlook to the job.

Since he was sworn in on January 5, Donelan has made a number of changes based on a vision of a cooperative relationship with staff and more direct involvement with inmates and their concerns.

When Donelan announced his candidacy for sheriff after four successful terms as state representative, Rice Flanders, one of my friends and a member of the Orange Democratic Town Committee, expressed shock and disappointment.

"He was doing so well as a state rep," she said. "I thought he'd go on to be a state senator and maybe even run for the US Congress. Why would he want to be sheriff?"

The answer to that is part practical, part philosophical.

On the practical side, consider that Donelan is very much a family man with a wife and three teenagers. There is the shorter car trip from Orange to Greenfield rather than Boston. The salary and likely security offered by the sheriff's position could be other factors.

Philosophically, Donelan is a follower of the John Adams school of thought advocating a citizen government with legislators serving for a while, then returning to a career or business. Donelan describes public safety work as his true calling.

Prior to heading for the state house as a legislator, Donelan served ten years as a police officer in Orange and South Hadley, followed by six years as a probation officer. His resume includes a bachelor's degree from Westfield State College and a master's of public admnistration degree from American International College, Springfield.

As sheriff, Donelan supervises the serving of papers related to civil law, but his primary responsibility is the county jail, which employs about 130 corrections officers and houses an average of 250 inmates. The jail has a capacity of 300 inmates, so the overcrowding that plagues many prisons is not usually an issue.

While there are occasional fights and other negative behavior and thus the need to segregate certain individuals temporarily, the jail is not burdened by violent felons or gang-related conflict, even though there are a few gang members behind bars there.

When Donelan began making daily visits to the pods, as residential units are called, the inmates were quite surprised and appreciative. They can also observe the sheriff eating prison food, which he does most days.

Donelan said personnel issues sometimes emerge, including layoffs due to budget cuts and technological advances, but he has made it much easier for employees to gain access to him. To remove a figurative wall between him and his staff, he simply ordered that a previously locked door become unlocked.

The new sheriff says he feels fortunate to head an organization with a very energetic and well-trained staff. "I want to define the culture that we're all working together," he said, adding,

> I have accomplished more in these first few months than I anticipated, mostly because there was a real desire on the part of the staff for strong leadership and a new direction. I have had a lot of support and acceptance.
>
> For inmates, the emphasis is on job training, counseling and mental health treatment.

From previous community work, Donelan knows that many people locked up for misdemeanor violations have spouses and children back home in Orange, Athol, and more than twenty other towns, and his vision involves a future where men can go home, improve their lives, and play a positive role in the community. More than eighty percent of the inmates have had substance abuse issues, indicating that such problems must be dealt with on the community level as well.

To prepare inmates for return to successful family life, the Athol-based PATCH agency conducts a fatherhood program for inmates.

The new sheriff is also building relationships with communities and providing assistance to towns with inmate work crews. He supports the study for a county wide emergency dispatch service, and he would like to establish county-wide animal control and a training program for local police officers.

Published in *Athol Daily News,* May 12, 2011
Copyright © 2011 by Newspapers of Massachusetts, Inc.
Used with permission.
Update: after fourteen years as Franklin Country sheriff, Chris Donelan retired on January 31, 2025.

Robert Perkins, Newspaper Techie, Is Retiring
2014

I'm not sure whether it's good news or bad news for Bob Perkins's wife of fifty years, Monika, but having just turned seventy-two on January 4, he is retiring later from his job as the *Athol Daily News* production manager.

For half a century, Bob has been intimately involved in the technical aspects of putting out a daily newspaper. Over that time, the technology has changed so much that if one were to count the sheer number of machines once working at the newspaper and then replaced by new machines, it would run well into the hundreds.

The most obvious change in the newsroom has been from typewriters to computers, but digital technology has made many advances and continues to do so. As a result, it was only a few weeks ago that new hardware and software came into the newsroom. The old Quark software system couldn't be upgraded, and the switch was completed to a newer program called InDesign plus the use of cloud, off-site storage of data.

Editor Deborrah Porter commented, "He was happy to see his final project take place with this conversion. That was his vision, and he saw it through."

My first job at the *ADN* was not writing, though Editor Barney Cummings did accept a few freelance pieces. The part-time job offered to me in the mid seventies by Perkins was Friday night typesetter.

Typesetting was done on a machine with a keyboard and yellow paper tape punched by me without benefit of a screen so errors could be corrected only later. The tape was fed into a device that used light to expose photography-grade paper and thus create the image of type as indicated by the tiny holes my machine made in the tape.

Bob, who had grown up on a dairy farm in Petersham, began working at the *Athol Daily News* in 1964 when he was twenty-two years old. One chore was taking papers off the press as they were printed, and he also was trained to be a Linotype operator.

The *ADN* was then located at the corner of Island and Main streets, and the printing process involved hot type, a molten lead alloy formed by brass matrices of the loud clickety-clacking Linotype machine. A flatbed press produced the newspaper.

In 1971, Perkins worked with his colleague, the late Harley Smith, to transform the newspaper's production into the digital age. Harley was a pioneer at utilizing computers. In 1960, he worked with the IBM Sabre system for reservations at American Airlines' Bradley Airport operations.

ADN publisher Richard Chase, Jr., commenting on Bob's retirement, said, "He saw a lot of change, switching from Linotype to Compugraphic in 1971. That was a sea change for us, and we were following the trend of newspapers that were abandoning hot type and going to computer typesetting."

Bob must have a vivid memory of a single day in 1971 when the *ADN*, with all the equipment, relocated to its current Exchange Street building.

The Compugraphic system involved a five-foot tall machine with a maximum capacity of one megabyte of data, Chase noted. Today's digital capacity is in the realm of gigabytes and terabytes, words I learned to use myself only in the past year or so.

Bob and Harley worked together on another important evolution in the 1980s, as the paper had abandoned the flatbed press for the web press. Working as a team, they figured out how the web press could be used to print books. It was tricky and complex to lay out the pages in a configuration that would allow them to be cut and bound into a book.

The newspaper, the smallest in the state, was partially sustained financially by the printing of town reports for more than a hundred Massachusetts towns. My first local book, *North of Quabbin: A Guide to Nine Massachusetts Towns*, was printed on the web press. I had become a full-time reporter for the *ADN in* 1979, and Bob and other colleagues helped make my book a reality. The book, inaugural project of my now defunct Millers River Publishing Company, went through two printings, a total of about seven thousand copies.

Another important change, completed in 2013, was a modernization of the production of aluminum plates that go on the offset web press. Scott Crowl, pressroom manager, collaborated with Bob to purchase a direct computer-to-plate system replacing the previous computer-to film-to-plate system.

Office Manager Judy Monte, who worked with Bob on aspects of production and office chores, praised him for his helpfulness. "He was always available when you needed him," she said.

The newspaper will not be hiring a replacement for Bob, and his responsibilities will be divided among several staff members, including Jared Robinson, Theresa Cody, Crowl, and Jessica Gale-Tanner.

I decided to write this column as a surprise for Bob, so I haven't had a chance to ask him what his plans are for the future. I'm sure that he'll keep busy. Monika probably has a few ideas.

Published in *Athol Daily News,* January 9, 2014
Copyright © 2014 by Newspapers of Massachusetts, Inc.
Used with permission.

Meet Walker Korby of Trustees of Reservations
2010

Walker Korby
photo courtesy of Walker Korby

Walker Korby, North Quabbin superintendent for the Trustees of Reservations, works hard taking care of some of the most scenic properties in the region.

At thirty-four, the Erving resident and skilled naturalist brings to his work and to the community broad-based training, an unbridled sense of adventure, and some passionate ideas about how different life will be in the not too distant future.

When I interviewed him in the early afternoon one Monday, he had been up for hours, having been awakened at 4 p.m. as a volunteer Erving firefighter, called to a blaze on Lake Mattawa in Orange.

When I called the previous week to set up the interview, he had just returned from Martha's Vineyard, where he was on a crew undertaking a prescribed burn using fire as a land management tool, on a Trustees property there. As a trained wildland firefighter, he has traveled with the Massachusetts wildfire crew to Idaho, Montana, Arizona, and Alaska.

Working for the Trustees since 2007, he is responsible for eleven properties reserved for public enjoyment: Brooks Woodland Preserve, Swift River Reservation and North Common Meadow in Petersham; Jacobs Hill, Doane's Falls, and Royalston Falls in Royalston; Elliot Laurel Reservation in Phillipston; Bears Den in New Salem; Redemption Rock in Princeton; Dexter Drumlin in Lancaster; and Mount Warner in Hadley. More information can be found at thetrustees.org

A big part of the job is supervision of the Tully Lake Campground in Royalston, which received six thousand visitors in the 2009 May-October season.

Acquiring an education for himself and then defining himself as an educator, Korby says, "My passion has always been connecting people with the rest of nature. We are part of the environment that we live in."

Korby hails from Red Bank, New Jersey, and received two degrees from UMass, Amherst—a bachelor of science in natural resource studies with minors in anthropology and wildlife and a master of science in geography.

As a high school student in New Jersey, "I met my mentor," Korby said, referring to a Jon Young, founder of the Wilderness Awareness School, wildernessawareness.org. Young learned from author Tom Brown, Jr., who had been trained by Stalking Wolf, an Apache elder.

Those specialized teachers focused on primitive skills, earth living, and animal tracking, all with the intention of developing a deep connection with the natural world. When Young's programs were presented at Korby's high school, Korby, well on his way to becoming an Eagle Scout, concluded, "This is what I want to do."

One of his most fascinating educational experiences was a 28-day program at the Boulder Outdoor Survival School in the Escalante River region of Utah. Walker was one of a dozen students, guided by two instructors, who completed the 275-mile wilderness course. It began with a four-day impact hike with no tent, no sleeping bag, no food, and no water.

Korby described how he and the others ate nothing for four days "except for some cattail pollen" and drank brown, red, green, and cloudy white water whenever they found it, filtering it through a bandana and then adding some aerobic oxygen drops to kill bacteria. Later, there were caches of food en route, including a surprise treat of bananas hanging on a juniper tree.

He drew a short straw one day and thus was the one who had to wield the knife to slaughter a sheep—"a powerful experience," he said, recalling his tears falling into the pit dug to catch the blood. To this day, he is not squeamish about such things, recently helping some friends in Montague who grow their own chickens to slaughter and dress the flock for the winter's supply.

In recent years, Korby has taught nature courses at secondary schools in Greenfield and for Greenfield Community College, including the "24-Hour Experience" pioneered by retired GCC professor Larry Buell, and ancient wilderness living skills taught at Buell's Earthlands complex in Petersham.

Among his adventures in Idaho was tracking wolves, introduced there at the same time the controversial predators were introduced to Yellowstone National Park.

Korby is committed to a "passion for developing community resilience." With the arrival of "peak oil," where extraction of oil is no longer economically viable, and the current economic downturn with persistent high joblessness, Korby believes that people will learn to share more and become more interdependent. The convenient way of life that many have become accustomed to will no longer be viable, he predicts.

As if to set an example, Korby sometimes takes the bus from Erving to his office in Athol's Millers River Environmental Center.

A different lifestyle lies ahead, with a social infrastructure including elements such as the North Quabbin Time Bank, already in existence—see nqtimebank.blogspot.com, Korby believes. His ideas offer clues to optimism in hard times.

Published in *Athol Daily News,* November 24, 2010
Copyright © 2010 by Newspapers of Massachusetts, Inc.
Used with permission.
Update: Walker Korby left the Trustees and became a full-time firefighter with the Turners Falls Fire Department. He also got married and began a family.

Congressman Jim McGovern: A Passionate Man
2011

US Representative Jim McGovern addresses a group in Greenfield Town Hall.
photograph courtesy of *Athol Daily News*

"Give us a vote! Why won't you give us a vote! Let us have a vote so we can do what's right for the American people."

That was Jim McGovern speaking, seen on a YouTube video, his arms going up and down above the podium in the United States Congress.

Our region is about to have a new representative in the United States Congress, a passionate man named

Jim McGovern, a Democrat from Worcester—and every indication is that he will serve us well. Following the approval of district borders with Massachusetts going from ten to nine reps, McGovern began to familiarize himself with towns new to his bailiwick–to be known as the Second Massachusetts District. He may or may not have a Republican opponent, but it's unlikely any challenger will oust the popular eight-termer.

Jim came to the King Philip Restaurant in Phillipston for a meet and greet organized by Orange Democrats. The event was open to everyone, and the lounge at Craig Twohey's popular eatery was a perfect venue offering comfort, informality, and free appetizers. Craig's late father, Paul Twohey, a committed Democrat and dedicated educator, would have been proud of his son's graciousness.

Prior to arriving in Phillipston, where he spent more than two hours, McGovern appeared on Athol-Orange Community Television during its auction.

He was traveling with his aide, Kathleen Polanowicz, the designated staff member assigned to hear the concerns of constituents.

McGovern is not a puffed-up personality type and didn't work the crowd as if to make an impression as many politicians do. Rather, he seemed very relaxed and simply made himself available to people. He was very approachable and listened attentively. No one monopolized his time, giving everyone a chance. In just five minutes, I told him about my own concerns, including land protection, health care, education, tax reform, civil rights, nuclear energy, and peace. Before departing, McGovern spoke briefly and pledged to be a frequent visitor to the region so he can keep up with people's needs and desires. He respectfully paid tribute to United States Congressman John Olver, who is retiring. McGovern showed awareness of the value of small-town and rural communities, including his enthusiastic support for small-scale agriculture. He showed great concern for both veterans and uniformed military personnel while also advocating withdrawal from Afghanistan and favoring a foreign policy that stresses diplomacy over military action.

Before his election to Congress in 1996, the fifty-year-old McGovern spent fourteen years working as a senior aide for the late US Representative John Joseph Moakley, D-South Boston.

Since his election, he has been widely recognized as a tenacious advocate for his district, including help for small businesses, saving police jobs, and aiding regional transit. He said he'll be an advocate for extending commuter rail service further west.

During his eighth term in Congress, McGovern serves as a senior minority whip; the second ranking Democrat on the powerful House rules committee, which sets terms for debate and amendments on most legislation; and a member of the House agriculture committee.

McGovern is also co-chair of both the Tom Lantos Human Rights Commission and the House Hunger Caucus. McGovern has also been successful in bringing federal funds to his district.

More information about Jim's family life, education, and career – including lots of YouTube videos—can be found on his website, mcgovern.house.gov.

Published in *Athol Daily News,* November 22, 2011
Copyright © 2011 by Newspapers of Massachusetts, Inc.
Used with permission.

Athol's Last Iceman Shares Some Memories
2018

Athol's last iceman, Ronald Legrand, 84, has vivid memories of a lifetime of hard work in a traditional New England industry replaced a long time ago by modern technology. While I am wistfully dubbing him "the last iceman," there probably are some others in the Commonwealth who are veterans of businesses that provided homes with ice from local ponds.

Ron invited me to chat with him and his wife, Marilyn, in the spacious kitchen of their beautifully refurbished old farmhouse on Waite Road in a remote part of Athol near the Petersham town line. The son of Eugene and Ellen Legrand, Ron was born in that house.

Eugene had come to Athol from the South Hadley-Holyoke area in the 1920s, purchasing an existing ice-harvesting business from a Mrs. Taylor. Ron's five siblings, Frances, Faith, Joyce, Lester, and Eugene, Jr. were all involved in aspects of the Athol Ice Company, but he is the sole survivor.

"Here's a gift for you," he began, handing me a yellow card, seven by eleven inches, that was commonplace in Athol homes all through the early twentieth century and before that. Placed in the window of a home, the card signaled the iceman how large a block to deliver and place in the home's icebox.

Icebox was a common word in the home where I grew up in New York's Catskill Mountains—and all over the USA. For many years after my parents acquired an electric refrigerator, probably in the early 1950s, my mother would instruct me after a meal to put the perishables "in the icebox."

The Athol Ice Company, owned by the Legrands, cut huge three-hundred-pound ice cakes, as they were called, on the pond located near the intersection of Fairview Avenue and Chestnut Street. Ice houses adjacent to the pond and another one at Lake Ellis, both used for year-round storage, were torn down decades ago.

Athol historian Dick Chaisson wrote a detailed article, published in the *Worcester Telegram & Gazette* on February 2, 1969, about the Legrand ice business, which I highly recommend to readers who want to know more. I chose it for the opening piece in Chaisson's 1985 anthology, *Hometown Chronicles,* published by my Millers River Publishing Company and out of print but available on the used book market. His article includes a detailed description of ice-cutting that Chaisson found in an 1886 edition of the *Athol Transcript* newspaper. Harvesting ice was a complex and often dangerous task involving horses that dragged sharp blades along heavy planks to score the ice in a perfect grid to prepare for cutting—initially with hand tools and later with power saws.

Ron's father lost most of his fingers on one hand because of an accident involving a power saw, and Ron showed me a discolored portion of his hand revealing remains of an injury caused when it was pierced all the way through by the sharp end of a pair of tongs. He said it happened on Thanksgiving morning when he was a seventh-grader and recalled being "taken to Dr. Grossman's house, and he patched me up."

High school boys as well as college students home for winter vacation were among the dozens of workers hired during the peak season. One of them was my former *Athol Daily News* colleague, fellow Columbia alumnus, and friend (also a former teacher and selectman), the late John Casella.

While the Legrand business and its competitor, City Ice on Sanders Street, served local homes, there was ice harvesting elsewhere in New England serving millions of city dwellers. In his research on the lost Quabbin towns, local historian J. R. Greene learned that huge ice houses, most on Greenwich Lake, flooded with three other Massachusetts towns to create Quabbin Reservoir, supplied ice for the New York area and beyond with much of it shipped via the former Athol-Springfield railroad known as Rabbit Run.

Ron recalled that in the 1950s as the ice business was winding down, he began working for Temple Oil Company, delivering fuel and doing oil burner installation and repairs.

Family life means a lot to the Legrands, and a sign in the kitchen says Nana and Papa's Nest Where the Flock Gathers. Their daughter Karen died at age 42, and the flock consists of Legrand children Kris, Kurt, Kimberly, and Kay Ellen plus eight grandchildren and seven great-grandchildren, all of whom live in the area.

Thanks to Athol barber Kent Roussel, who cuts my hair and Ron's, for suggesting this as a topic for "Inside/Outside."

Published in Athol Daily News, February 1, 2018
Copyright © 2018 by Newspapers of Massachusetts, Inc.
Used with permission.

Update: Ronald Legrand died in 2022.

Remembering Joyce O'Lari,
Veteran Athol Daily News *Reporter*
2010

Joyce Edith (Manning) O'Lari worked as an *Athol Daily News* reporter for decades—longer than any reporter in the paper's history—and she had a stellar reputation for accuracy and fairness.

I enjoyed being her colleague at the newspaper for ten years and was encouraged by the managing editor Deb Porter and the publisher Rick Chase to write about her as part of the newspaper's seventy-fifth anniversary series.

She died after her 1990 retirement from the paper in a fire at her home on Chester Street in Athol on August 11, 2002. She was seventy-seven and had lived a full life, though her final years were difficult as she was pretty much confined to her home with an oxygen tank, needed because of advanced emphysema.

The fire made for bold headlines, but her tragic death should not be allowed to overshadow a life filled with hard work that benefited the *Athol Daily News* community. She led a rich family life with an array of friends and relatives who remember her good nature and sense of humor.

Joyce was born in Athol on February 7, 1925, the daughter of Maurice and Cora Guilmette Manning.

She grew up in town and graduated from Athol High School, Class of 1942. She helped chronicle the many changes that the town and region experienced through the second half of the twentieth century and often shared memories about "days gone by."

She was very much a small-town girl and seemed impressed with my many travels, while I was equally impressed with how rare it was for her to leave the Athol-Orange area. One Monday, after I told her I had been to Brattleboro and Northampton over the weekend, Joyce exclaimed, "Boy, you really get around!"

Marcia Gagliardi, who worked alongside Joyce as a reporter before she left the *Athol Daily News* and became a teacher at Athol High School, recalled Joyce telling stories about the dances in Wheelerville, where the Italian immigrants—including Gagliardi's mother's family, who ran a convenience store where the Wheelerville Club is now —got together on Saturday nights and put the children to sleep on benches while they socialized, drank, and danced.

A member of one of those immigrant families, Albert "Bat" O'Lari, married Joyce on August 9, 1943, in Las Vegas while he was serving in the US Army. They lived most of their married life in Athol. In the summer of 1968, the couple was honored by 175 friends and relatives at a silver wedding anniversary party at the Elks Hall in Orange. The Talk of the Town band played for dancing, and Eric Witty was master of ceremonies.

At the time of the anniversary, Bat was working as a form grinder at UTD Corporation. He died in 1977. A few years later, Joyce became a frequent companion of Pep Erali, himself a widower.

Joyce began her Daily News career as social reporter from 1944-1950, a period when women in journalism generally did not cover real news. Times change, and the social notes published daily in those days are no longer part of *Daily News* coverage. She took a few years off to raise her children and was hired in 1960 as a general assignment reporter, a position she held until her retirement thirty years later.

Gagliardi described her as

certainly the mainstay of the newsroom, a very capable reporter. I particularly remember the attention to detail, and it was Joyce who tutored me (and all of us) in Associated Press style. She and Chuck Stone had a particular camaraderie, as they had been part of the staff for a long time.

John Casella, who worked alongside Joyce in the latter years of her career, wrote a tribute to her in 1997 after she retired. He stated, "The town officials and office workers thought the world of her. They liked and trusted her. For a town hall reporter, that is most unusual."

Joyce spoke almost daily to certain people in town, including funeral home personnel such as Mary Lou Schwab of Murphy's Funeral Home. Schwab, who was also in charge of the Athol branch of the Red Cross, helped arrange for Joyce to receive an outstanding media award in 1980 at the Red Cross Northeast Region headquarters in Needham for her work publicizing blood drives.

Aside from praising Joyce as a reporter, Schwab said, "She was a very nice person," and added, "She was also very dedicated to her husband."

On the occasion of Joyce's death, the Athol Board of Selectmen honored her with a public tribute by board member Joe Maga. He said that as a reporter "she showed decency, honesty, and integrity—and was never afraid to ask the tough questions."

Dick Chaisson of Athol was a reporter for the *Athol Daily News* briefly and then had a lengthy career as Athol bureau chief for the *Worcester Telegram and Gazette.* He sat with Joyce through many meetings over decades. At the time of her death, Chaisson said, "We've lost a sweetheart, a great lady, and a good reporter. She was very careful with the facts."

More recently he commented, "She is still close to my heart. She was a lot of fun. We shared a lot of laughs and serious stuff, too."

Gagliardi recalled how Joyce would often crosscheck facts with Chaisson, whose paper, of course, was considered the competition, so Joyce had to do that "in a clandestine way, because if Barney (Cummings, the editor) knew, he would screech, and occasionally he would know."

One of Joyce's most useful skills, helpful to me, was her ability to cope with Cummings, the often volatile editor of the paper. Joyce's grandson Albert O'Lari, an Athol police officer, lived with her for much of his life, and they were especially close. That closeness started when Albert was quite young. According to Albert, Cummings sometimes stopped by Joyce's home from time to time, and "they would shoot the (expletive) and yell at each other. He'd scare the (expletive) out of me, and I'd hide under the table until he left."

Albert, now living in a new residence built on the site of Joyce's burned out house, is the son of Joyce's older son, Richard, and his wife Patricia. At age twenty-one,

Albert moved in with Joyce upon the death in 1995 of her younger son, Robert, age forty from a brain tumor. Albert said both he and Joyce needed company at that time in their lives.

Albert recalled that Joyce had an "open-door policy" at her home where friends and family could come to "borrow money, burn a butt, or have a drink." Albert encouraged me to write about all of Joyce's varied interests and traits, including the fact that she liked to drink and smoke and laugh at a bawdy joke, all linked to an atmosphere filled with love and sociability.

She loved music, with Neil Diamond as a favorite. She enjoyed reading and had a strong interest in current events, with newspapers and clippings always piled here and there. She liked good food and would often take Albert to the King Phillip Restaurant in Phillipston for baked stuffed shrimp. "I ate like a king with her there," he said.

Albert said Joyce knew he always wanted to be a cop, and she paid for his college education.

Childhood memories cherished by Albert and his sister Jeanna include summer vacations in a rented beach house at Old Orchard Beach, Maine, and other occasions when Joyce drove the two of them to Maine just to see the sunrise and walk on the beach. Jeanna also remembers her grandmother giving her big coloring books and putting her artwork up around the house.

Albert recalls Joyce leaving the house for outings with "the red lady," identity unknown, in a convertible—a scene that reminded him of the fictional movie characters *Thelma and Louise.*

Albert said that, at her request, he didn't call her Grandma but rather just Joyce. She told him, "It's hell to get old, and I don't want to feel old."

In Joyce's house, Albert recalled, he did not have total freedom, as she did not allow overnight stays with his girlfriend, Naomi Parker. He said, however, Joyce wasn't totally strict about this, and, when he broke the rules, Joyce let him know by singing a tune made popular by Gordon Lightfoot, "Sundown, you better take care if I find you been sneaking down my back stairs."

Regarding bawdy jokes, one of Joyce's favorites involved an annual phone call from Bill Clark of Royalston, an *Athol Daily News* employee for a while. Each year on May 1, starting in the 1960s and continuing for decades, Bill telephoned Joyce to say, "Hooray, hooray, the first of May, outside playing starts today." (Except the actual word he used was not "playing.")

I thought it was pretty funny, and so after I left the paper, I took up calling Joyce at the end of the day each May 1 just to ask her, "Have you heard from Bill Clark yet?"

The answer was always "Yes," and then we both enjoyed a good laugh and the phone chat.

I called Bill at his Florida home to verify the story, and he added that, since Joyce's death, the annual phone call has been going to Joyce's granddaughter Jeanna, who also appreciates the playful joke.

Clark's recent comments about Joyce Edith, as he always called her, started with talk about their clowning around and ended with this:

> She never missed a good story, and she never sensationalized a good story. She did an excellent job as a reporter. I admired her from day one. You'd think she wasn't getting it all, but she was absolutely elegant.

Published in *Athol Daily News,* May 8, 2010
Copyright © 2010 by Newspapers of Massachusetts, Inc.

Used with permission.

Two Local Artists: Michael Humphries and Ami Fagin
2011

Many people have artistic talent, and many of them produce beautiful works of art and could thus be called successful, but only a small percentage find a way to make a living using that talent.

There are several such artists in the North Quabbin region. For more than two decades, I've been aware of the work of two of them, Michael Humphries, a woodworker, and Ami Fagin, an illustrator.

Michael Humphries
photo by Leigh Youngblood

Humphries's custom work was featured with extensive photography in a *Boston Globe* article. The article recounts how Salem-based architect Peter Pitman designed custom cabinets and contacted Humphries to create them.

The article says:

> The condos at Lewis Wharf occupy granite warehouses built in the 1830s and retain such glorious features as exposed brick walls, soaring ceilings, and hefty fir beams. To create focal points as well as necessary storage areas in the newly combined unit, Pitman designed an abundance of built-in cabinets and hired Northfield-based woodworker Michael Humphries to make them.
>
> Inspired by the look of nineteenth-century Biedermeier furniture, the pieces are made of tiger maple, also known as curly maple, stained to a golden hue and detailed with black.

Humphries explained that maple is "a great juxtaposition with the old honey-colored beams."

Built-in bookshelves in the study and a bow-front entertainment center in the living room feature beading made out of walnut that was dyed dark—less expensive to do that process than to buy ebony or another exotic wood.

Founded in the 1970s, Humphries's business was based on White Road in Warwick until 2010 when, as the result of a divorce, he relocated his residence and all his machinery and crew to Northfield. He has plans to build a new home in Warwick in the near future.

The *Globe* article was not the first time Humphries got media attention. I wrote about him in the *Athol Daily News* in 1985, and his beautiful multi-hued cutting boards were featured in "The Alpha Kitchen" collection in the May 2010 issue of *Playboy* magazine.

While much of Humphries's work is done for clients in Boston, Nantucket, New York and beyond, some of it has been installed locally, and he has some items for sale on his website. They are not Made-in-China bargains but the work of a fine artist and craftsman, so they don't come cheap. Humphries was born in 1947 and spent his youth in Pennsylvania. He majored in English at Haverford College near Philadelphia and obtained a master's in education at UMass, Amherst. The artistic instincts were strong, and after a modest start in his Warwick barn, Humphries built a significant business.

Ami Fagin
photo courtesy of Ami Fagin

A similar shift in direction took place with Ami Fagin, who grew up in Newton, studied horticulture, and received a degree in international agricultural development at UMass, Amherst. Her talent as an illustrator moved her at first to create cards and do stenciling in homes (including mine), but before long, she established Twentieth Century Illuminations as her art-centered business and, like Humphries, successfully used the Internet to reach clients.

She lived for a time on Orange's Tully Pond with her husband, Wayne Hachey, a contractor specializing in artistic tile work. They live in New Salem with their son, Austin, a senior at Northfield Mount Hermon School.

Fagin's primary product in recent years has been Jewish wedding certificates called ketubot with calligraphy in Hebrew, featuring intricate watercolor, gouache, and India ink artwork. She also makes English-language wedding certificates with varied wording.

She is immersed in a complex and emotionally draining project called Beyond Genocide. About two-thirds completed, Beyond Genocide is defined by her as "an emerging series of twenty-four contemporary illuminated manuscripts exploring the legacy of genocide and mass annihilation around the globe."

Essentially a traveling show, Beyond Genocide includes workshops and collaborative academic and cultural programming available along with installations in museums, galleries, and schools.

Technology plays a major role in Fagin's work. She does original artwork by hand, records it as a digital file on her computer via a flatbed scanner, and then creates amazingly high-quality prints. Computerized images allow her to alter text and create custom items sought by clients.

Published in *Athol Daily News*, August 25, 2011
Copyright © 2011 by Newspapers of Massachusetts, Inc.
Used with permission.

Update: Michael Humphries retired from his woodworking business. He married Leigh Youngblood, and they reside in Warwick. Ami Fagin continues her career as an artist, including frequent contribution to *Uniquely Quabbin* magazine. Her series Beyond Genocide has a permanent home at Keene, New Hampshire, State College.
Her website is 20thcenturyilluminations.com.

Meet Nellie Melaika,
Grand Dame of Athol's Lithuanians
2018

Nellie Melaika and Scott Pralinsky
photo courtesy of Scott Pralinsky

Kucios is the traditional Christmas Eve dinner of Lithuanians, and I think I first became aware of Nellie Melaika when I saw her name in the *Athol Daily News* as one of the people helping with the celebration at Saint Francis Roman Catholic Church.

I was introduced to her in person at a community event when she was in her mid-eighties, and I remarked to myself, "Nellie Melaika is the grand dame of Athol's Lithuanians." She still helps with kucios but gives most of the recent credit to Marie Ann Shatos and Jackie Dougherty.

At ninety, Nellie lives on Hamlet Street in a downtown Athol neighborhood long populated with Lithuanians, the largest European ethnic group to emigrate to Athol in the early twentieth century. She resides in the same home where she lived as a child with her parents,

Lithuania-born Casimir and Apolonia Melaika. The American Lithuanian Naturalization Club, once a focus of education for immigrants, as well as Saint Francis Church, are nearby.

Nellie has not let aging stop her from being active and vibrant. Last week, my friend Scott Pralinsky brought me to her home where we ate some watermelon and engaged in lively conversation. Scott calls her Aunt Nellie, stemming from the fact that she and Scott's mother, Barbara Bennett Pralinsky, who died recently, were best friends since their childhood when they were neighbors.

Sitting across from Nellie at her kitchen table, I enjoyed viewing her expressive face as she talked about her life then and now—all of it constantly peppered with laughter.

At one point, referring to her successful aging, she told me that "a good night's sleep is the best medicine," and when I said, "Laughter, too," she agreed—and laughed some more. She also credits good eating habits with her longevity, and until recently, she went to the Erving Senior Center for aerobics classes. Her mobility has been somewhat impaired by a vision problem related to macular degeneration, so she gets around with a walker.

As for sleep, Nellie said, "I go to bed between twelve and one, so I don't like to get up early." She remains close to family members, especially her sister, Janice "Jan" Sidman, "who calls every day to make sure I'm okay."

Nellie expressed gratitude to two nephews, Robert and Matthew Brookman, sons of her sister Jan from a previous marriage, who help with her care so she can remain in her own home. Catholic Charities provides assistance, too.

Nellie is a 1945 graduate of Athol High School. Her first job was helping Father John Jutt at Saint Francis with secretarial chores, including typing up notes the priest took during pastoral counseling with couples.

"Boy, did I learn a lot!" she exclaimed with a grin. Later, she was a clerical worker at Cass Toy Company and the LS Starrett Company, where she did a lot of Xeroxing. She said the women in the office usually wore skirts, but one time, on a cold snowy day, she came in with slacks and some co-workers "made a big thing of it, exclaiming 'Nellie's got slacks on!'"

She served as president of the now-defunct Mount Grace Association of Business and Professional Women, belonged to the Athol Memorial Hospital Auxiliary, and was a Town of Athol elections poll worker.

Work and play constituted the main things in Nellie's life, and she never married, explaining, "I never met the right one." There were many men she liked who danced with her, however, when she went polka dancing with women friends to places such as the Quonset Club in Amherst and Maronas Park in Worcester. Nellie recalled being somewhat keen on "one guy who played in the band," adding, "Son of a gun, I couldn't get him. His loss." More laughter.

She also enjoyed swimming, sometimes going to First Tully, one of several swimming holes in the Tully River off North Orange Road, as well as to Hampton Beach, New Hampshire.

Nellie speaks, reads, and writes in the Lithuanian language and once visited that Baltic Sea nation with a Boston-based group. She had a good time, but she did not connect with any relatives as the trip did not include the area that was her "rural and poor" ancestral home.

Scott has been friendly with his adoptive aunt since his childhood and recalled the time that she traveled with his family to Mexico, reminiscing, "I remember you liked a margarita."

Nellie laughed and said, "Those are good! We had a good time down there!" She added that nowadays, she occasionally will have a glass of Michelob Light, and friends sometimes delight her with a Mocha Frappuccino from Starbucks as a gift.

Published in *Athol Daily News*, July 26, 2018
Copyright © 2018 by Newspapers of Massachusetts, Inc.
Used with permission.
Update: Nellie Melaika died on October 4, 2023, at age ninety-six.

A Backhoe, a Bulldozer, and Many Stories to Tell
2012

Ron DeJackome steps off an excavator
photo by Bill Forgues

Ron DeJackome is a man with a backhoe, a bulldozer, and many stories to tell.

When he told me a few of those tales, some involving considerable danger, I thought of the proverbial cat who has nine lives.

Aside from a backhoe and bulldozer, Ron also has an excavator, a front-end loader, and a triple-axle dump truck, all part of his business as a self-employed excavation contractor based at his home on White Horse Lane in Petersham. As assistant fire chief, he sometimes drives Petersham Fire Department vehicles.

He launched his own business after working for most of the 1970s for B. L. Frye, Inc., of Orange. All of Ron's equipment, valued in the hundreds of thousands of dollars, was accumulated over time with the help of bank loans and some good deals at Brookside Equipment Sales, Phillipston.

When I purchased land and set out to build a house with several friends in Royalston in 1973, one of our first needs was an excavation contractor, and we chose B.L. Frye. The twenty-seven-year-old equipment operator was Ron, who did a great job.

Another example of Ron's artistry with big machines is the granite block partial foundation of a restored carriage house erected in Petersham. We reconnected at that site, and we reminisced. He told me some of his adventures and accomplishments—well beyond the routine of foundations and septic systems.

Included was his service in his early twenties as a US Navy radioman with top secret clearance. He was on the aircraft carrier USS Essex in 1968 when a Russian bomber crashed in the Norwegian Sea after buzzing the ship. US authorities sent a video to the Soviet Union to prove the plane was not shot down. If you Google "USS Essex and Russian TU-16 crash," you can see Ron at 1:34 in the two-minute YouTube clip.

In the summer of 1969, a time when others were enjoying Woodstock and celebrating the first walk on the moon, DeJackome was a petty officer in charge of Navy security and intelligence in a very dangerous place—Danang, Vietnam.

Ron heard wartime bombs, but he also has experienced dynamite explosions as an excavati\ on contractor. He encountered dangerous incidents with dynamite while digging a well at the home of local spiritualist Elwood Babbitt near the Northfield-Warwick line and at other work sites, including the road to the Mount Grace summit.

While working for B.L. Frye in the 1970s, Ronnie was operating a backhoe to excavate ditches in order to direct the Erving Paper Mill's wastewater to a new treatment plant. A railroad flagman did not perform his duty as pre-arranged, and Ronnie narrowly avoided serious injury when a westbound train came down the tracks, screeching to a halt.

On another occasion, while removing snow from the parking area of the Rodney Hunt Company in Orange, Ron's backhoe hit the nearby railroad tracks, and he was knocked unconscious in the cab. An Orange firefighter came by and woke him up before the situation worsened. Trucks with brake problems were another cause of scary experiences for Ronnie. Heading for Diemand Farm in Wendell with a newly purchased second-hand truck that had faulty brakes, he sped downhill, but then a steep uphill grade was a lifesaver. In another case, driving a fire truck on Route 101, Ronnie had to veer off into the woods in order to avoid a collision when brakes failed.

Ronnie did excavation related to the installation of the septic system at the Brotherhood of the Spirit dormitory in Warwick and gained some insights into life at the controversial commune.

The quirkiest story of all concerned the burial of twenty pregnant cows killed by a lightning strike one August day on the Perkins farm in Petersham. Ronnie was hired to dig a huge grave for the unlucky bovines, but in the summer heat, the cows were already decomposing, resulting in the loud hissing of escaping gas and an unimaginable stench.

At sixty-four, DeJackome is faring well and enjoying his work, his camp on a pristine lake in Maine, and family and community life. Ronnie has been married to the former Charlene Waid for forty-two years. The couple has two sons, Jason, 39, a Massachusetts environmental police officer, and Adam, 36, a Connecticut corrections officer, and four grandchildren.

Published in *Athol Daily News,* February 23, 2012
Copyright © 2012 by Newspapers of Massachusetts, Inc.
Used with permission.

Tom Kellner creates an ice sculpture, top
photo by Lynne Kellner

Linda Ruel Flynn pauses during a work session in her studio
photo by Sandra Costello

Noteworthy Visual Artists Tom Kellner and Linda Ruel Flynn
2016

The visual arts vary widely in style and media as reflected in the appealing creative work of two area residents, Tom Kellner of South Royalston and Linda Ruel Flynn of Athol.

Tom, who does his work in his studio as the Millers River rushes by, is primarily a sculptor, using marble and other natural stone as well as wood and clay. His ice sculptures, formerly created for Worcester and Northampton First Night events, have been a feature at Starry Starry Night, the annual New Year's Eve celebration in Orange.

He also does paintings. In fact, I recently got the idea to write about Tom when my friend Kate Collins of Royalston showed me a watercolor she just did of Mount Monadnock—as viewed from a field near her Royalston home—and told me that she and Tom had just worked side by side viewing the mountain, each interpreting the view in a work of art. Another friend, Rice Flanders of Orange, has a Tom Kellner painting of the Millers River in her home, perhaps not a coincidence, since they both live adjacent to the river and are both active with the Millers River Watershed Council. Tom's versatile creations reflect an eclectic approach, including a portrait bust in stone, a limestone fireplace, and submarine structures in plate steel.

"Art is a tool of transformation," Kellner says,
> both personal and political. The transitions in my life inform my art as it evolves to reflect changing perspectives. When my daughter was born, for instance, she inspired a series of sculptures reflecting the birth process.

He added, "My goal is to create art that presents a context in which the creator—and the viewer—interact with it and respond to it."

A native of New Jersey, Tom completed a liberal arts program at Holy Cross College, Worcester, majoring in economics, but when he took a few art courses, his life took a turn. He relocated to the Boston area and taught classes in various media to youth at the Cambridge Community Arts project in the late 1970s.

He then went to UMass, Amherst, working in the foundry with bronze and acquiring a master's degree in sculpture. After graduation, he worked for eighteen years in human services, including time at the Fernald School in Waltham, which overlapped with a return to the arts. Tom was working in East Boston doing marine salvage when he and his wife, Lynne, decided it was time to leave the city and buy a house. They started looking in Concord and ended up buying a home on North Main Street in Orange, but soon after that, they spotted an ad in the *Athol Daily News* for a house in South Royalston. The Kellners were the first to respond to the ad, buying the house and renovating it over time and transforming the barn into a studio.

Tom taught for twenty-five years at the Worcester Art Museum, but starting in 2016, he worked at Fitchburg

State University, teaching "all sorts of things, from drawing to ceramics, 3-D Design and portraiture."

Tom's wife, Lynne, whom he met at UMass, has had a long career as a professor of psychology at Fitchburg. The couple has been married for thirty years, and they have two grown children, Marissa and Brendon, both living in Boston.

Tom acquires marble from Vermont and limestone from North Adams, and he has milled logs for wood creations.

Tom remembers working together with Linda Ruel Flynn at the former Orange Art Center "quite a while ago," and was impressed from the beginning by the mural she painted at the New Salem Country Store. She painted part of a mural at the Athol Hospital cafeteria.

Linda's creative space and retail store, dubbed Flora-ly, is in Room 333 at the Orange Innovation Center, OIC, 131 West Main Street, Orange. She has a website, flora-ly.com, which states, "We are a sweet studio specializing in artisan flower preservation."

Flowers from every event can be preserved, Linda explained, and artistically framed with accompanying text.

It is done without chemicals, using just "pressure, time and air." She creates collages—all one of a kind—using herbs and flowers, especially Dusty Miller, hydrangeas (her "absolute favorite"), larkspur, bee balm, dahlia, peonies, Queen Anne's lace, roses, and more.

She considers Flora-ly a second-generation business started by her mother in Ashburnham as Lydia's Pressed Flowers.

Preserving flowers with personal meaning, such as those for weddings and funerals, is key to

Flora-ly. As Linda sees it, "It is an honor to create something that holds a memory." She is finishing up a commission from the Mount Grace Land Conservation Trust in preparation for the organization's thirtieth anniversary celebration.

Linda also paints, mostly abstract images from landscapes. "I love skies," she said. I have purchased many of her floral greeting cards, which are especially nice for personalized messages, including condolences and thanks. She says it's best to make an appointment by phone, (978) 895-0560 or email, linda@flora-ly.com.

Linda has lived in Athol with her husband Jim for more than twenty years, coming from Pittsfield. The couple has two grown children, Keegan of Burlington, Vermont, and Kendra of Boston.

Published in Athol Daily News, January 14, 2016
Copyright © 2016 by Newspapers of Massachusetts, Inc.
Used with permission.

Royalston Assessor Gets Assessed on the High Side
2015

"My big thing, really, is fairness," stated Jim Richardson of Royalston, who has served on the town's board of assessors for twenty years. Referring to the assessors' office in Whitney Hall, South Royalston, where the board meets twice a month, he added: "I really believe that when you come through the door there, you'll find that we are treating everyone the same as the next guy."

Jim Richardson takes a break with his wife, Barbara, and their grandchildren.
photo courtesy of Barbara Richardson

Assessors are important town officials to everyone who is a property owner because they play a role in calculating our real estate tax obligation. In my hometown, Royalston, residents have been fortunate to have three board members take care of things effectively and with a minimum of complaints.

Jim's colleagues on the board are Steven Chase and Michael Lajoie. Not long ago, the editor of the Royalston town newsletter, Beth Gospodarek (who is married to Steven Chase), mentioned Jim as one of the town's unsung heroes. Today's column is devoted to him along with Jim's wife, Barbara, former town clerk.

"Jim holds the assessors' office together," stated Steven. He added:

> It amazes me how Jim always maintains his humor and composure in the face of difficult problems or dealings with ornery taxpayers. Many towns have trouble filling assessors' positions. It takes someone with a strong sense of civic duty. The position requires schooling and certification from the state. The pay, about fifteen hundred dollars a year, probably (at least in Jim's case) works out to a couple dollars an hour.

Jim, a Royalston native, joined the board in 1995 when he was appointed to fill a vacancy, and he's been elected without opposition numerous times. It's mostly on-the-job training, Jim explained, though he got a good start with a brief course given by the Massachusetts Department of Revenue at Holyoke Community College.

Royalston has about twelve hundred parcels of land including some five hundred houses, and Jim notes that one of the biggest projects back in the 1990s was going door-to-door and reviewing every one of them. For a time, a few taxpayers complained about allegedly higher assessments from a view tax, but Jim says there is no such thing. "It's against the rules," he stated.

The board receives about six requests a year for tax abatements, and most of them are "plain mistakes and easily corrected." When abatement is denied, it can go to an appeals court, but "we have had only one appellate case in the twenty years I've been here, and we won," Jim said.

Jim likes the job while saying "maybe I could do better," and after twenty years of service, he'd be happy to train a new person who might be interested. Years ago, much of the job involved paper, but computers have become prominent. Jim credits the board's current clerk, Marie Mello, with being especially helpful and adept with technology. Driving a truck for Porter Transportation of Tully, a sand and gravel distributor, is Jim's day job since 1989, and it's something he loves doing. He commented:

> I'm a truck freak. I love trucks, starting in elementary school. I knew I was going to drive truck then, and when I got out of high school, I knew that's what I would do, and that's all I ever done.

Jim has delivered gravel for me and my neighbors, skillfully dumping a single load in three different places. The trucks he drives are super clean. He takes them home to wash and wax. He confesses, "It is a sickness almost. When you have a clean vehicle and clean windows, you feel better."

John Drew, president of Porter Transportation, said,

> You can't find a more honest and more trustworthy person. He is one of the better truck drivers in our region, very dedicated to his job. I don't have anything bad to say,

that's for sure. I leave him in charge of my business with no problem and total confidence.

Jim has a commercial driving license and a hoisting and engineering certificate from the Massachusetts Department of Public Safety which authorizes him to use a loader and excavator.

Prior to his current job, Jim was a self-employed truck owner-operator, driving a box trailer "just about everywhere," including trips to Texas and Arizona, hauling paper and plastic items and often sleeping in the truck.

Family life includes his wife, Barbara, and two sons, Mike, 21, who is employed at Pete's Tire Barn, and Aaron, 24, who works for Asplundh Tree Service. The Richardsons, married for twenty-eight years, are dedicated parents and enjoy their first grandchild, too.

Barb and Jim met in Northfield after Jim's mother moved there from Royalston. Barb was working at a diner. "He used to come in, and we struck up a friendship," she said, adding that it was years ago. Barb waitressed for nineteen years at Jeannie's Lunch, Templeton, and cooks and serves at the Royalston Country Store Thursdays and Fridays. She works at the Phinehas Newton Library in town Mondays and Tuesdays. She also served as town clerk for thirteen years.

"Royalston has been a good home to us," Barb said, and as a Royalston resident myself, I will add that the couple has been good to our town.

Published in *Athol Daily News*, May 14, 2015
Copyright © 2015 by Newspapers of Massachusetts, Inc.
Used with permission.

Duo Travels to Alaska and Back on a Harley-Davidson Road King
2016

Paul Thibodeau and Charlie Chase pause at roadside establishment Gold Panner during their seven-week trip to Alaska.
photo courtesy Paul Thibodeau

Marjorie "Charlie" Chase and Paul Thibodeau of Frye Hill Road, Royalston, have returned to their jobs and peaceful back-road home life after a seven-week cross-country motorcycle trip to Alaska.

The eleven-thousand-mile journey on the couple's 2014 Harley-Davidson Road King included a stop at

Niagara Falls, where they crossed into Canada and experienced a very complete search by the authorities—possibly due to Paul's beard and tattoos. The couple marveled at the dramatic scenery of the Canadian Rockies, where a kindly Mountie stopped them for a minor violation but let them go with only a verbal warning. Charlie commented that the weather was cooperative most of the time, except once in an unpopulated area at an elevation of about eleven thousand feet above sea level, when "we got caught in a tremendous storm that pummeled us with cold rain and there was nothing to do but keep on going."

Arriving at Anchorage, Alaska, they visited Paul's sister, Michelle Hall, who treated them to a jet plane flight to Barrow, the northernmost town in the state. Paul had a special reason for going there. He explained:

"I have a penchant for skipping stones—across lakes, rivers and oceans—and I needed the Arctic Ocean." He noted that he keeps track of where he has done it all around the perimeter of the USA and Canada from the Maritimes to the northern Pacific Ocean.

On the return trip, Paul and Charlie spent some time hiking in the American Rockies, finding them "very peaceful and serene."

Both recently divorced, the couple met in the early 2000s, and motorcycle riding became central to their friendship and romance. Paul recalled "it did take a lot of convincing" to get Charlie on the back of his bike.

The couple enjoys looking back on a hot August Sunday afternoon when, in their early days of biking together, they got caught in a thunderstorm. A bolt of lightning struck the road, and the rain was coming down hard. Paul turned around to check on Charlie, "and she had the biggest grin," he said, "so I knew right then and there that she was the one."

The current bike belongs to both of them, Charlie declared pointedly—"I own the back, and he owns the front." She doesn't drive the big machine herself.

The Royalston property where I interviewed them includes a comfortable old farmhouse and a barn where Charlie keeps two horses. She is a Spanish teacher at Narragansett Regional School, Baldwinville, and he works as a case manager at the Fitzwilliam, New Hampshire, Veterans Victory Farm while continuing his studies at Fitchburg State University.

Charlie, who spent her early years in Athol, is a graduate of Bethany College, Bethany, West Virginia, and also holds a master's degree from the State University of New York at Stony Brook. She is the daughter of retired *Athol Daily News* publisher Richard Chase Sr. My friendship with Charlie, who is fifty-six, began in the 1980s when her father asked me to edit her dispatches from Africa where she was traveling to visit Peace Corps volunteer Beth Gospodarek, who later married Charlie's brother Steve.

The word adventurous best described Charlie back then, and it remains one of her most admirable qualities.

Paul is certainly Marjorie's kindred spirit. He grew up in Worcester, where he experienced a difficult childhood following the untimely death of his mother. He started riding motorcycles at age sixteen, joined a riding club, and did not pursue higher education until many years later. My impression is that Paul was once a bit of a bad boy who still loves his bike but also is content writing poetry, studying hard, and cooking for Charlie. Now fifty-four, he is working on a master's degree in mental health counseling at Fitchburg State, where he also was awarded a bachelor's degree. Before that, he obtained an associate's degree from Mount Wachusett Community College, Gardner. It was a pleasure earlier this week, enjoying the warm late summer breeze in the twilight hour, to hear about their adventures while sitting behind their house on an attractive brick patio they recently completed themselves.

Published in *Athol Daily News,* September 22, 2016
Copyright © 2016 by Newspapers of Massachusetts, Inc.
Used with permission.

*Remembering Gene Bishop and Herman Goldfarb,
Two Doctors and Activists for Peace*
2020

Gene Bishop, MD, left, and Herman Godfarb, MD
Gene Bishop photo courtesy of Andrew Stone
Herman Goldfarb photo by Diane Keijzer

Every time I read about a monument erected to honor soldiers, I remember conversations I've had with friends about the need we feel for a monument of some sort to acknowledge those of us who were soldiers of a different sort—marching against war, specifically against the Vietnam War.

Most followers of *Rag Blog* are aware of that anti-war movement, a central pillar of the legendary Sixties, and this article is a memorial tribute to two activists, both of whom were also medical doctors. Both died recently, and linking them in this article is part of my own process of mourning for them.

They are Gene Bishop, MD (1947-2020), and Herman Goldfarb, MD (1927-2019).

Their deaths have impacted me because I had long-lasting and important friendships with both. Herman was also my cousin, and my relationship with him began when I was a child. I met Gene more than a half-century ago when we were both active in New Left circles.

Though the two doctors never crossed paths and were unaware of each other, I was struck by the fact that a twenty-year gap in their ages didn't matter much when it came to their devotion to peace and their compassionate professional and political work as left-wing doctors serving communities in need.

Herman, who was a member of the Communist Party, CP, starting in his youth in the 1940s, represents the activism and values of the Old Left, while Gene belonged to the Students for a Democratic Society, SDS, and was an archetypal New Leftist.

Gene Bishop, MD

My relationship with Gene began in the 1960s when both of us were involved in the underground press movement. Gene wrote for the Old Mole, a publication based in Cambridge, Massachusetts, where she had been a Radcliffe student. I was on the staff of Liberation News Service, LNS, which started in Washington, DC, and then moved to New York City. Several *Rag Blog* staffers have their own unique connections to LNS, and I had the pleasure of joining them at the Rag Reunion in 2016.

A year after graduation from Radcliffe, Gene married Dicky Cluster, her colleague in SDS and the Old Mole. Then, as part of their New Left pathway, Gene and Dicky went on the first Venceremos Brigade as volunteer sugarcane cutters in Cuba and wrote about their experiences for LNS. Their relationship lasted about three years.

Gene decided to pursue a career in medicine and was accepted to the Stony Brook University Medical School on Long Island, graduating in 1976. She chose to become an internist—primary care physician, and completed her residency at Cambridge City Hospital in Massachusetts. Board-certified in internal medicine, she settled in Philadelphia and served patients there for nearly forty years. Her second husband, Andy Stone, MD, has worked as a psychiatrist, recently helping veterans suffering from post-traumatic stress disorder. They had one child, Sarah Sky Bishop-Stone.

Gene's funeral at Mishkan Shalom Synagogue was attended by three hundred people, an indication of her impact on others. One of the main points made at that event was her role as an educator, including the steady stream of entries in the Caring Bridge website established for people who have a serious illness and want to keep in touch with a large number of friends and acquaintances.

Essentially, though it's hard to come right out and say it, her Caring Bridge entries were the narrative of an individual headed for an almost certain death in the near future. With an honest evaluation of her ups and downs, she discussed her medical condition as well as her mental state, her engagement in writing projects and current politics. She kept at those Caring Bridge entries right up to the last week or so, when her husband and daughter made the final posts.

I reached out to four individuals who knew Gene to share their thoughts, as follows:

Lucy Candib, MD

One of the things I will always remember about Gene is that she was always ahead of everyone else: pulling diverse women together to establish a free women's health clinic in Somerville over the course of a couple years, succeeding in the early seventies. She also walked faster than anyone else I ever traveled with. We went to Europe together one summer, and she was ten paces ahead of me all the time. I was always running to catch up. Likewise, she saw things coming politically sooner than other people and was always on target in identifying threats to women, low-income people, and people of color. One of the most astute political people I will ever know. I will miss her enormously.

Michael Ansara

When I met Gene Bishop, she was either a first-year or second-year student at Radcliffe. As you probably know, in those days Harvard maintained a separate college for women. By design, it accepted far fewer female students than Harvard did male. They lived in their own dorms, had their own graduation, and were not allowed to use all of the libraries that were open to men.

Gene became involved in SDS. Early on, she was part of the first collectives of women and was an early feminist—forcing many of us men to confront the sexism that was as endemic to SDS as it was to the larger society. When we formed the Old Mole, our new left underground newspaper, she was essential to its publication for two years and was a key leader in the women's collective at the Old Mole.

Gene was a person of commitment and powerful, if muted, passion. She was acutely aware of the unequal treatment of women and determined to change it in every aspect of her life. After she went to Cuba on that first Venceremos Brigade, our work took us in different directions, and then, of course, she went off to med school and we largely lost touch. I was delighted to see her last year for the first time in many years—and am very sad to learn she has died.

Carmen Febo de San Miguel, MD

I met Gene in the late 1970s when she joined Hahnemann Family Medicine Residency Program as attending physician. She had recently arrived in Philadelphia joining our program and, very importantly for me, joining the physicians at the Spring Garden Family Health Services Center where I was acting as medical director. The health center, associated with the family medicine residency program where I had recently completed my training, provided primary care to a poor, multi-ethnic community that primarily consisted of poor whites, African-Americans, and Puerto Ricans and other Latinos, as well as being a teaching site for residents in the program.

Gene was a breath of fresh air. To receive another female physician to our faculty, but one with such strong convictions for high quality of care to all, for her understanding, knowledge and experience of feminism and health care for women, was horizon-widening for me. I had graduated from medical school at the University of Puerto Rico, and although my heart and inclinations were in the right place, Gene's clearer experience and verticality of purpose provided a mold that helped me shape my own understanding and career path into the future.

Furthermore, Gene introduced me to women's music, including Holly Near, the Philadelphia-based Anna Crucis Choir, and many other memorable experiences I would not have gotten to know. But I can also claim that I introduced her to Puerto Rico. Visiting Puerto Rico together was very special for me, as I think it was for Gene.

Barbara Rothkrug, RN

When I left Liberation News Service in early 1971, I moved to Boston where the women's movement was in full swing. I moved in with Gene, who, with a group of friends, was organizing a health center run by women in two storefronts in Somerville, Massachusetts. (Gene had quit the Old Mole and gotten a job as a pulmonary function technician at Boston City Hospital). The center was to have all women staff, including doctors and mental health professionals. Everyone who volunteered there became a doctor or nurse, including me. So I owe my career as a nurse to Gene and the women's health center.

Gene became a lifelong friend, even though we lived far apart. She could put into words what I was feeling even when I could not. Even when she was terminally ill, she thought of other people's needs and tried to help out. Her openness about her own feelings was amazing and unusual. She continued her fight for better health care, dragging herself to conferences and demonstrations when she could.

More than a doctor, Gene's role as an educator and writer remained central, as she wrote articles for medical journals, some of them related to her own declining health. She had received radiation treatment for lymphoma when she was eighteen, and that was identified as the cause of her lung cancer. Her last major piece of writing went to the readers of Philadelphia's daily newspaper, The Inquirer, on February 18, 2020. It was updated online when she died. It is entitled "Radiation cured her cancer 55 years ago. Then it ended her life."

Gene loved the outdoors, especially hiking, and like so many New Leftists, eventually developed an interest in environmental politics. She wrote:

> In 1979, 14 years after my treatment, the worst domestic nuclear power accident in US history occurred at the Three

Mile Island nuclear plant in Pennsylvania. I was more than sympathetic to the nuclear disarmament movement. And although I understood that nuclear war and my radiation treatment were considerably different, I did begin to wonder if the treatment could have had unexpected consequences.

Herman Goldfarb, MD

The politics that filled the life of Herman Goldfarb reflects a different era from the one that affected Gene but included many of the same values. Herman's children prepared the following obituary published in newspapers near his home:

Herman was born on June 29, 1927, in the Bronx to first-generation Jewish immigrants from Russia, Rose and Irving Goldfarb. Being raised during the Depression shaped the rest of his life and solidified his social activism and commitment to civil rights. He fought for these beliefs throughout his life, from his early days as a union organizer, through the sixties and seventies when he protested the Vietnam war.

As a staff doctor at Community General Hospital in Monticello, New York he picketed in solidarity with the hospital workers when they went on strike in the 80s. As recently as two months ago, he was outside Planned Parenthood, showing his support for reproductive rights.

He was a brilliant man whose deep curiosity and scientific wonder led to a lifetime of learning and deep appreciation for the natural world. He began his career as a chemical engineer, but luckily for many residents of Sullivan County, became a doctor, moved to Monticello and began his long career giving medical help, advice, and love to all his patients. His political convictions had him following world affairs until the end. He felt he had done all he wanted in life, and his only regret was that he couldn't be here to see how it all turns out.

The repressive politics of the McCarthy era—named in the late 1940s and throughout the 1950s for Wisconsin Senator Joseph McCarthy and his Red Scare, referring to Communists who in slang were called Reds—influenced Herman's life in many ways, because he was in fact a Communist and all Communists were targets—with many in party leadership ending up in jail or in exile.

Herman's decision to go back to school to become a medical doctor was a direct result of the McCarthy era and its demand for loyalty oaths required in many professions and pledging to uphold the US Constitution without membership in so-called subversive organizations, especially the Communist Party during the McCarthy Era. He had difficulty holding down a job as a chemical engineer. He got his medical degree from the Albert Einstein College of Medicine in the Bronx, followed by a residency at Montefiore Hospital, also in the Bronx. He was an internist and a pulmonologist.

Herman was warm and loving to me as I was growing up, and he visited our home often, always bringing gifts meant to improve my intellect. He once told me that he brought girlfriends to meet my parents because he wanted their approval.

As I matured, he shared more of his political biography with me. He joined the CP as a youth and was very proud of his participation in rallies and a student strike at City College of New York, CCNY, in the late 1940s. A *Wikipedia* entry entitled "Knickerbocker Case" tells the story about the strike, part of a campaign against Professor William E. Knickerbocker because of his alleged anti-Semitism. The article notes,

CCNY alumni continued to commemorate the 1949 strike, which for many students marked the beginning of their political involvement in progressive causes and in civil rights.

Herman, age twenty-two at the time, was one of them.

During the McCarthy period, when Julius and Ethel Rosenberg were arrested, tried, convicted, and then executed in the electric chair for allegedly providing the Soviet Union the "secret of the atomic bomb," Herman teamed up with other scientists in an effort to prove that there was no such "secret," given what was available already in scientific journals. Obviously, the effort was to no avail, and the Rosenbergs were executed. The Rosenberg case was a traumatic event for America, but especially for CP members.

He sometimes voiced criticism of the party leadership. He told me that he won a generous scholarship to attend Massachusetts Institute of Technology, MIT, but the party wanted him to go to CCNY to be among the working class.

Herman had flaws, as humans do. He definitely was a typical macho man, and that trait led to his divorce. His machismo made me anxious when I decided to come out to him as a gay man. I was so relieved and forever grateful when he immediately expressed his love and support—and educated himself about homosexuality.

Calumny is the word that came to mind as I was mulling over plans to write this article. Here's the definition from dictionary.com: "the making of false and defamatory statements about someone in order to damage their reputation."

Both the Old Left and New Left have been subject to despicable examples of calumny, especially in regard to the Vietnam War and the counterculture but also earlier in regard to Communists. Fine human beings like Gene and Herman are a testament to the injustice of such defamatory statements.

It's true that Communist Party loyalists were badly misinformed and perhaps foolish in their admiration of Stalin, except perhaps for seeing the Soviet Union as an essential wartime ally against the Nazis and Fascists. Some Old Leftists, followers of Norman Thomas (disliked by the Communists), were wiser on that score. We New Leftists had our own flaws, but the negative characterizations about both Old Left and New Left have taken up a lot of ink. It takes some work, in this arena, to emphasize the positive, and that's what The *Rag Blog's* frequent history articles strive to accomplish.

I wrote the following in my autobiography, *Left, Gay & Green: A Writer's Life:*

> People in the labor movement joined the Communist Party because of the party's strong commitment, both ideologically and in practical terms, to workers' rights. Furthermore, the CP took a strong stand against anti-Semitism and against the racist Jim Crow laws in the American South. The party held a strong position, at least in theory, on equality for women, and I first heard the term "male chauvinist" as a child when my mother used it to describe the bad behavior and attitude of some men she knew, though I don't think she leveled that charge at my father. Without success, the CP advocated for socialized medicine, but in the same era, Franklin D. Roosevelt's New Deal Congress adopted some of the proposals pushed by the CP, most notably the Social Security system. The CP grew to at least fifty thousand members in the 1930s, but by the 1950s the numbers had dwindled to fewer than ten thousand. My parents remained among the steadfast few.

As for the New Left, its members are maligned in many ways, but none of the anti-war activists I have known, including Gene and Herman, ever spit at a soldier returning from Vietnam, and yet that ugly myth endures. Check out *The Spitting Image: Myth, Memory, and the Legacy of Vietnam* by Vietnam veteran and sociology professor Jerry Lembcke, published in 1998.

The hard work of the peace movement, including teach-ins on so many campuses, and reaching out to GIs via coffee shops and special periodicals, not to mention the huge mass actions, are unappreciated.

We've been disrespected in a way that simply obliterates the reality of kind, compassionate, thoughtful people like Gene Bishop and Herman Goldfarb.

The renowned and influential psychologist Bruno Bettelheim (1903-1990) was particularly nasty in attacking the young people of the Sixties in his speeches and writings. A 1970 *New York Times* article states,

> For millions of Americans who are understandably nervous about the radical young, the Bettelheim view of what ails them seems both timely and important: many of the hippies, militants, Yippies, and assorted fringe groups of the New Left, he believes, are emotionally sick . . . What is even more disturbing to Bettelheim is that an influential segment of the adult world has elevated this sickness to the status of a "youth culture," glorifying what should properly be looked upon as a pathology.

Many articles in later years accused our generation of choosing the bourgeois life, or "selling out." An anonymous writer in American Dissident took aim at the youth of the sixties with this:

> They wanted to change the world, but they simply changed ideas instead. Today they want to change jobs, cars, or TV sets. That's all. They were separatists, hippies,

Maoists, organic foodies, feminists, peace and love, Marxist-Leninists, and finally New Wave. They became young or old yuppies full of horseshit.

The writer created a list of famous so-called sellouts including Abbie Hoffman, Bill Clinton, Hillary Clinton, Tom Hayden, Jane Fonda, Eric Clapton, Mick Jagger, Dennis Hopper, Bob Dylan, Allen Ginsberg, and Gary Snyder.

Particularly offensive to me was his description of Ginsberg, a devoted pacifist, for "becoming, a tenured professor and worried not of ideals but of his own paltry fame and place in the established-order literary canon."

The piece concludes:
> The counterculture, as it was called, was really nothing but a lightly disguised arm of corporate America dressed in paisley, smelling of patchouli oil and incense, yapping in hippie jargon while selling, selling, selling, always selling.

Well, few alumni of the 1960s protests actually became wealthy, and the amazing good work that Gene and Herman did all through their lives was never motivated by greed. In fact, greed, selfishness, violence, cowardice, and prejudice were the aspects of society they fought to the end.

previously published in the *Rag Blog*, theragblog.com

Discretion, Valor, and the "Good Liberal"
2013

The October obituary of Ralph Dungan, one of President John F. Kennedy's top aides who later served as ambassador to Chile, reminded me of my one-time experience with that man referred to by a historian as a "good liberal."

In the mid 1960s when I was living in Santiago, Chile, on a scholarship from the Inter-American Press Association, I was called in to Ambassador Dungan's office along with an American graduate student and given a tongue-lashing that I have never forgotten.

My friend and I both had strong objections to growing military involvement of the United States in Vietnam and awareness of the growing anti-war movement back home, and we had been expressing our views to our Chilean friends. Fluent in Spanish, I spoke to a gathering of students at the University of Chile.

In the most patronizing tone, Mr. Dungan said if we opposed US policy, we should "return to the US and run for Congress." He made veiled threats that if we continued the behavior, our lives could become complicated.

I became quite angry about his lecture and considered informing Chile's very popular left-wing press. That could have led to headlines, but the truth is that

I was quite intimidated by the whole thing. I was only twenty-five years old, and I was afraid I could lose my scholarship and my related draft deferment. I didn't stop expressing my views, but I became more cautious.

Thus, a classic liberal showed his true colors on the issue of the Vietnam War and freedom of expression. And I was not as courageous as I might have been. Looking back on my entire life, that moment in Chile is the best example I have of truly understanding the famous line from Shakespeare's Henry IV: "Discretion is the better part of valor."

previously published in the *Rag Blog*, theragblog.com

The Strange Short Life of Minerva Mayo
2012

 Minerva Mayo (1803-1822), who lived her short life in Tully and North Orange, was not an ordinary early-nineteenth-century farm girl. She described herself as a rogue, and the very fact that she saw herself as a writer, putting down her thoughts and observations on paper starting at age sixteen, makes her unique.

 The exact cause of her death at eighteen is unknown, but it is quite possible that she took her own life, according to Jack Larkin, the Old Sturbridge Village, OSV, director of research who has studied Minerva's writings and who came to Orange in the late 1990s to probe an example of microhistory. He calls Minerva "troubled, divided, intelligent, and doomed."

 I stood at Minerva's gravestone in North Orange Cemetery and pondered what I had just read, Larkin's OSV document entitled "'To Leave My Parents Mourning Here': The Life and Death of Minerva Mayo of Orange, Massachusetts."

 The writings of Minerva are contained in thirty-four pages of a small school exercise book entitled "The Life and Writings of Minerva Mayo by Herself." The book, assembled by relatives after her death, includes an autobiography, letters, and poetry.

We learn in Minerva's own words about her rebellious ways. She writes, "As soon as I was large enough to run out of doors, no one could keep me indoors without confining me." Her mother, Sally Mayo, who spent much of her time weaving, restrained Minerva by tying her to the loom. Minerva added, "I have often had to feel the rod of correction for endeavoring to run from my mother . . . out of doors."

Minerva liked the idea of wearing trousers rather than frocks, and one of her hobbies was whittling, usually done by boys. One time, the five-year-old Minerva was whittling and accidentally put out her little sister's eye with a knife. A few years later, she saved that same sister from drowning. "Father said to me," Minerva wrote, "you have done well; you have now paid the debt you contracted in putting out your sister's eye by saving her life."

Her father, Calvin Mayo, was more tolerant of her and kept her mother from doling out harsh punishment, as he tended to favor only "mild words" to express his displeasure. One time, however, when Minerva was only four, she joined him while haying but became rowdy and upset, screaming "so loud I was heard near a mile." Her father then "placed a large stone on my back . . . until I became very submissive."

Discussing Minerva's writings with North Orange history buff Glenn Johnson, I learned that Calvin Mayo dug the canal from Tully River into Packard Pond. The Minerva Mayo document was first brought to my attention by my friend Nina Barszcz, who owns a house on Packard Pond with her husband, Frank, so I enjoyed that link, and the following one, too.

One of the letters was written by Minerva for a neighbor, Mrs. Hannah Collar, as Minerva identified her, and that caught my attention, as Collar Brook, named for that family, is a Tully River tributary that flows through my land. The impoverished Mrs. Collar had been abandoned by her husband and children. The letter that Minerva wrote for Mrs. Collar was a plea to her son to take care of her so she wouldn't have to live her final days "under tyranny" of a Mr. Baker with "the town's poor some of which are ugly and foolish and all of a dirty pack."

Death and tragedy seemed to be much on Minerva's mind as well as religious ideas. At that time in the history of Orange, conflicting versions of Christian theology had emerged. Minerva's family was in the camp of the Universalists, who developed the concept of universal salvation rather than focusing on eternal damnation. One of Minerva's poems said:

"Young as we are we may decay

Our souls to live in endless day."

Minerva wrote in gory detail about a carriage accident that occurred on Aug. 30, 1820, just after the sun "bowed beneath the stupendous hill" (Tully Mountain). A woman was killed and "the road was stained with her blood." She also described the "whirlwind" that killed two residents of Orange on September 9, 1821. When the tornado came through, she wrote, "despair was in every bosom, mothers weeping over their children." In her account, Tully Mountain blocked and ended the tornado that had begun in Northfield.

Minerva, gripped by unhappiness, planned to escape to Ohio wearing her brother's "great coat and hat." It's unclear from the writings but plausible that she left and then returned, ending her life in Orange. She left a poignant farewell note to her parents.

Larkin, whose essay is on the OSV website, concludes that Minerva's writings are "a gift of sorts from Minerva to us, a posterity that she could not have imagined."

Published in *Athol Daily News*, Sept. 27, 2012
Copyright © 2012 by Newspapers of Massachusetts, Inc.
Used with permission.

Dental Hygienist Lynn Trinque Is a Dedicated Professional
2017

Lynn Trinque
photo by Diane Keijzer

For more than three decades, starting when she was not quite twenty years old, Lynn Trinque of Gardner has cleaned the teeth and helped maintain healthy smiles for hundreds of North Quabbin residents.

"I love my job," she said emphatically, showing her own smile and positive outlook already familiar to me because I've been her patient since the beginning of her career.

Fresh out of Quinsigamond Community College, Worcester, Lynn obtained her associates degree in 1986 and was hired by Emil Pauli, DMD, a young dentist who was then an associate of Dr. Paul Larocque in Orange. When Dr. Pauli launched his own practice in uptown Athol, she continued to work for him.

Only seventeen when she graduated from Narragansett Regional School, Baldwinville, she had already chosen dental hygiene for her life's work. Her own family dentist, Dr. Robert Latour of Gardner, did not have a dental hygienist, but Lynn was getting braces from an orthodontist, Dr. Frank Weisner, who had a hygienist. That's when she became interested in teeth, and around the same time, her high school English teacher, Robert Bellefeuille, suggested dental hygiene as a career choice.

Following her college graduation, she passed both regional and national board examinations, and right after that, Dr. Weisner advised her about an opening available in Orange. As Lynn put it, "Dr. Pauli gave an opportunity to a very fresh-out-of-school nineteen-year-old."

Lynn uses metal tools called scalers and curettes to remove plaque and calculus (tartar) that has formed on teeth, noting that "anything put in a patient's mouth is either disposable or sterilized" in an autoclave.

The cleaning procedure, technically called prophylaxis or preventive treatment, regularly includes checking blood pressure and pulse, an evaluation of periodontic (gum) health, x-rays, and checking for oral cancer. Dr. Pauli allows an hour for the hygienist to do her work and for him to check the patient, too. Regulations require her to work for a dentist under indirect supervision for x-rays and prophylaxis, meaning the dentist does not need to be present, but under direct supervision for local anesthesia, meaning he must be present.

Part of the job is educating patients about how to maintain good oral health, Lynn said, explaining that "oral health is part of a whole-body approach." She pointed out that ailments such as heart disease and diabetes, as well as patients' use of medications, can be a factor.

"What about bad breath?" I inquired. She said that it can be due to diet or stomach issues as well as post nasal drip. Sometimes patients are advised to brush their tongues to help deal with mouth odor.

Lynn has always appreciated Dr. Pauli's "dedication to infection control" for both staff and patients. It includes universal precautions requiring use of gloves and face masks. Office equipment is kept up-to-date, and Lynn uses a loupe, special glasses for enlargement, to do her work. In order to maintain licensing she obtains twenty continuing education credits every two years. Two and one-half years ago, she learned to administer local anesthesia by injection, which she does occasionally. She belongs to the American Dental Hygiene Association.

The daughter of Frank and Chris LaFalam, Lynn was born and raised in Baldwinville. They continue to live in the house that was her childhood home. She has been married for twenty-seven years to Steve Trinque, her high school sweetheart, who became a professional barber. He owns and works in Pete's Barber Shop, located in the couple's Baldwinville home.

"I love spending time with my family and friends," Lynn said, adding that "my husband and I enjoy traveling." She teaches children's classes at her church in Baldwinville.

Summarizing her career, Lynn notes that she sometimes sees three generations of patients in the same family. She concluded, "I appreciate working with a dentist who is so dedicated to treating every patient as if they were a family member. I am grateful to work with the long-term, hard-working staff that is dedicated to the care of the patients."

Published in *Athol Daily News*, July 27, 2017
Copyright © 2017 by Newspapers of Massachusetts, Inc.
Used with permission.

Update: Dr. Pauli retired in 2024 for health reasons, and Lynn was compelled to seek work elsewhere.

Shrewsbury Native Dan Zona, North Quabbin Leader
2017

Dan Zona
photo courtesy of Athol Savings Bank

There's a fifty-two-year-old family man, an important North Quabbin community leader who has lived in Shrewsbury his whole life and spends most of his days hereabouts, not complaining a bit about his daily commute. His name is Daniel J. Zona, president and chief executive officer of the Athol Savings Bank, ASB.

I met Dan about four years ago when he authorized a hundred dollars for ASB sponsorship of my book, *The Man Who Got Lost: North Quabbin Stories*. But what made me decide to write a column about him was an experience I had last fall, when I took advantage of free shredding offered by ASB to the entire community to help reduce risk of identity theft.

When I pulled into the bank parking lot, Dan was among a group of employees helping put boxes of papers in the shredder. We had a nice chat, and I was struck by the fact that the bank president had vacated his desk to do some manual labor. Later, I spoke in confidence to a few bank employees I know asking them their opinion of their boss. Without exception, they praised his management style and treatment of staff. It's in my bones to reject elitism, and I wouldn't want to see ink wasted on a boss who doesn't treat employees well.

Dan has been the head of ASB for five years, taking over the helm from Sam Hokkanen, who also sponsored one of my books, Dan previously served in other senior management positions.

He graduated from the University of Massachusetts, Dartmouth, in 1986 and became a certified public accountant, "toiling" for eight years for the large Boston-based form, KPMG. Then he got a job with State Street Bank, commuting from Shrewsbury to Boston.

He doesn't mind commuting fifty miles each way from Shrewsbury to Athol, made easier by listening to satellite radio or audio books. He comes to Athol five days a week, sometimes six days.

Dan and wife, Marcia, have two daughters, Gabrielle, 20, a junior at Stonehill College in Easton, and Olivia, 17, a junior (and gymnast) at Shrewsbury High School.

ASB is defined as a community bank and Dan describes his job as "varied and wide-ranging." He clearly needs to know "a lot about a lot of things," he quipped. The bank has $400 million in assets, with $320 million in deposits from a range of customers—individuals or retail, commercial, municipal, and nonprofits.

One of the biggest challenges he and other bank leaders face is "continuing to manage regulatory oversight." Dan believes that there is a "disproportionate" burden on small banks when it comes to regulation, though he agrees some regulation is needed.

He noted that coping with regulations is time-consuming, pointing out that he relies on senior management and the entire ASB team to oversee all aspects of the bank from regulatory compliance, technological advancements, consumer and business lending, overall customer service, and community involvement.

Dan says the bank is aware of its competition, embraces it, and has to be innovative and nimble. He noted, "Society moves fast, the industry moves fast and Athol Savings has to move with it." The bank's staff includes information technology experts who assist with such services as online banking, mobile deposit, and bill pay. There's even online chat allowing customers to use their high-tech devices to ask questions and get answers. It's still okay to call on the phone and walk into the bank to speak to an officer or teller.

Dan recognizes that when a financial crisis struck the nation, "banks got a bad name," and he acknowledges that people in some of the large banks "took risks that community banks such as Athol Savings Bank didn't take." As CEO of the bank, Dan works with other managers and with the board of investment, a committee of the board of trustees.

Celebration in 2017 of the bank's 150th anniversary was on Dan's current agenda. Aside from the main branch in Athol in the gorgeous 1927 bank building, there's the convenience center off Exchange Street and the uptown branch (where I always enjoy a friendly chat with supervisor Donna Smith, who is smitten with her baby grandchild Isabelle). Other branches are located in Ashburnham, Baldwinville, Barre, Gardner, and Winchendon.

ASB employs ninety-one people. Dan believes in "organic" and "steady" growth and would love to continue expansion of ASB.

I heard rumors that the bank wanted to dispose of the old headquarters —expensive to heat and with reduced foot traffic–but Dan said the bank will maintain it.

"Job and family keeps me pretty busy," Dan said, responding to my question about "hobbies." Last year, however, daughter Gabrielle was in Florence, Italy, for an entire college semester, and Dan traveled there with his wife and younger daughter for some quality family time and appreciating his Italian heritage.

Published in *Athol Daily News*, March 23, 2017
Copyright © 2017 by Newspapers of Massachusetts, Inc.
Used with permission.

Is a Muralist a Contortionist? An Acrobat?
Read About It Here
2012

Many years ago, I was fortunate to have Ami Fagin of New Salem, a talented young artist, climb up a tall stepladder and paint some original stenciled designs on my bedroom walls. I continue to enjoy looking at them and explaining the symbolism to visitors. Something painted on a wall seems so much more permanent and even more personal than a painting you hang.

Sonja Vaccari of Royalston and Susan Marshall of Orange are two local artists I count among my friends, too, who specialize in painting murals.

Sonja's mural at the Maples, the home of Patience and the late Werner Bundschuh located on the town common in Royalston, is a jaw-dropping depiction of two places important to the Bundschuh family–Royalston and Charlestown.

Charlestown is depicted with the fabled Bunker Hill monument and the USS Constitution, "Old Ironsides," in the harbor and the gold-domed Statehouse in the background. On the opposite wall, Sonja painted the Maples as well as Royalston Town Hall and nearby church, while on smaller walls and alcoves, she painted familiar outdoor scenes, including Doane's Falls and wildlife such as a heron, a bobcat, and a black bear.

Sonja Vaccari pauses while working on a mural.
photo courtesy of Sonja Vaccari

Sonja has always painted and created, starting in her childhood, and more recently was mentored by Royalston artist Jack Kacian when they worked together for the former Holbek Group in Orange, creating exhibit designs for museums and other clients.

"Jack recognized my talents and offered me a job, then showed me some tricks of the trade," said Sonja.

She also worked on murals in the homes of Pierre and Marie Claire Humblet on the common and Pat Jackson on Old Winchendon Road. One commission involved eight weeks of work to paint a scenic mural in the rehabbed Weekapaug Inn, Westerly, RI.

The artist said she starts with ordinary interior flat latex house paint as the base, using acrylic artist paints for the rest. She can also create a mural off-site using canvas to be affixed like wallpaper.

Sonja hails from Natick and has lived in Royalston for twenty years with her husband, George. She has two sons Daniel and Jan and a daughter Andrea.

Sonja's website, sonjavaccarimuralist.com, includes photos and text such as this comment:

There are times when a muralist is really a contortionist. On any given job, I may be painting in a corner, stretched prone along a baseboard or sitting Indian style on the floor for days. You might find me perched on a ladder or lying flat on my back, atop a scaffold wielding a brush.

Ladders and scaffolds are also used by Susan Marshall, my other muralist friend, who calls herself an "acrobat artist." Susan and her husband, Ted, came to Orange in the early 1970s as part of the back-to-the-land movement and connected to the counterculture arts community. She obtained an interdisciplinary degree at UMass, Amherst, where she studied with the late Doris Abramson of New Salem in theater arts and Leonel Gongora in fine arts. She later did graduate studies at the Pennsylvania Academy of Fine Arts in Philadelphia.

After living in Orange for a decade, the couple relocated to a New Jersey suburb of Philadelphia, where Ted worked as a physical education teacher and coach and where Susan launched her own business in the

Susan Marshall stands near her "Welcome-to-Orange" mural at the former Orange Savings Bank.
photo by Paul Franz

decorative arts. For many years, she has done work in residences, commercial lobbies, and offices.

Sometimes her work involved travel and thus can be found from the Chesapeake Bay region to Lancaster County, Pennsylvania and in vacation homes on the Jersey shore and around Cape Porpoise, Maine.

Susan notes that she works closely with interior designers, explaining, "What I do is collaborative. It's about what the designer and the client and I come up with." One project was a mural in an Italian restaurant in New Jersey, featuring Tuscany towns she and Ted have visited.

She has donated paintings as fundraisers to the Mount Grace Land Conservation Trust in support of its land protection work. Images included the trust's Hidden Valley Conservation Area in Wendell and a beaver pond on conservation land behind the Marshalls' home.

Her floral images grace the homes of Orange friends Rice Flanders and Marcia and Paul Larocque.

Susan plans to embark on creative projects in her studio in Orange. The couple's daughter Jessica relocated to Conway with her husband. The couple also has two sons, Casey and Theo.

Published in *Athol Daily News*, December 6, 2012
Copyright © 2012 by Newspapers of Massachusetts, Inc.
Used with permission.

Update: Sonja has done outdoor paintings in Athol on the concrete remains of Stan's Body Shop. Susan lives full-time in Orange and has done outdoor paintings on several buildings in downtown Orange and on the new Fisher Hill School.

At Seventy, Petersham's Larry Buell Maintains His Environmental Vision
2014

Larry Buell hikes in Petersham.
photo courtesy of Larry Buell

Sometime today, Larry Buell of Petersham, age seventy, will go alone to a spot in the Swift River Valley where he had an epiphany exactly fifty years ago. As he ponders the future, he will spend a day and a night commemorating the environmental awareness he acquired in his youth.

The *Merriam-Webster Dictionary* defines epiphany as "a moment in which you suddenly see or understand something in a new or very clear way."

The date was March 21, 1964, and for Buell,

a quiet time in a beautiful part of Petersham, with clean water flowing in the Swift River, East Branch, helped him understand the way that all life is connected.

Following several years of advanced education and work as a teacher, Buell established a nonprofit called the Institute for Environmental Awareness, Inc. The institute soon created Earthlands on part of the old Buell farm on Glasheen Road. For several decades, Earthlands has offered workshops and a variety of gatherings focused on ecology, Native American culture, alternative energy and healing methods, growing food, nature-oriented ritual, social justice, and more. Some people made their home on the site and experienced intentional community living.

"For the Earth and all life." Those words, summing up his personal credo and world view, were chosen by Larry for the closing of a recent outreach letter about the future of Earthlands, which could be foreclosed if a buyer is not found. The property, with an off-the-grid lodge and forty-eight acres of land, could be listed with local Realtor Chuck Berube. Buell is hoping for a buyer that will pay four hundred thousand dollars and carry on Earthlands's mission and ethic.

Buell wants to start a new phase of his life and seeks to transfer Earthlands to new ownership, leadership, and management. There are many people who have already been involved with the unique organization featuring an intentional community and extensive environmental education.

The property is adjacent to hundreds of acres of forested land, part of the original farm, which has been protected with the help of the Mount Grace Land

Conservation Trust and the Massachusetts Division of Fisheries and Wildlife.

In his letter, Buell writes:

> My only role right now, is to search and welcome the next set of leaders and stewards who have the skills, passion, resources, and commitment to guide Earthlands to its next incarnation.

Buell, a native of the North Quabbin, refers often to the "sense of place" that colors his view of the unique region—and which I also embrace in my writing.

Following his graduation from Mahar Regional School in 1961, Buell studied for a year at Kimball Union Academy in Meriden, New Hampshire, and made plans to attend Wentworth Institute in Boston to learn carpentry. However, he shifted gears and attended Springfield College, where he played on a successful basketball team. In 1965, the team traveled around the world and was inducted into the Basketball Hall of Fame in 2013.

Attracted by the Civil Rights Movement of the mid 1960s, Buell joined activists in North Carolina to help register voters.

With his focus nevertheless more and more on the natural world, Buell obtained a master's degree at Pennsylvania State University and eventually earned a doctorate in education and environmental studies at UMass, Amherst.

He founded and directed the Outdoor Leadership Program at Greenfield Community College. The course he developed included the twenty-four-hour experience, assigning students to spend twenty-four hours in the wild. It was a precursor to the University of the Wild, an alternative higher education concept that Buell also developed. His travel to remote scenic parts of Siberia in 1991-1992 ushered in a more global vision that has influenced Earthlands's outlook.

The son of the late Harry and Ruth Beals Buell, Larry Buell experienced farm life in his youth. He married Carmen Buell in 1966, and they were divorced in 1987. Carmen Buell served in the Massachusetts legislature as a state representative and became an expert in health policy, later moving to North Carolina and heading up that state's human services agency. She retired from the position of chief executive officer of the Milbank Memorial Fund and resides in Manteo, North Carolina.

Larry filled me in on their two daughters.

Jennifer Buell Horschman lives in Asheville, North Carolina. She had lived for five years in Costa Rica, where she co-founded a Spanish cultural immersion program. Jennifer is 47 and has two sons, Nicolas, 12, and Henry, 11. Cynthia Buell Christian, 43, lives in Wilmington, North Carolina, where she works as an art teacher and is studying art therapy.

Larry plans to retire with his second wife, Katja Esser, whom he wed in 2012, to the eighteenth-century Buell farmhouse on Oliver Street near the center of Petersham. He will continue his work with the University of the Wild, finish writing several environmental and place-based related books and his own memoir, and engage in more research and programs on the history and landscapes of the North Quabbin region.

Published in *Athol Daily News*, March 20, 2014
Copyright © 2014 by Newspapers of Massachusetts, Inc.
Used with permission.

Abbey Plotkin: Her Good Heart Gave Out
2021

I wrote the following obituary at the request of family members, and family members and Abbey's friends told me they liked it a lot.
The family gave permission to include it in
From the Octagon.

Abbey Plotkin
photo courtesy of Charles S. Plotkin

Abbey J. Plotkin of Coconut Creek, Florida, formerly of New York City, died January 7, 2021 at the age of fifty-nine. Her good heart gave out, ending a lifetime of devotion to joyful dancing as well as her love of diverse friends and a large Jewish family.

Abbey was a professional dance performer and educator with a special interest in Latin American dance styles. She relocated from New York to Florida in November 2020 to continue her career. Friends and family admired her personal warmth and joie de vivre and also enjoyed watching her experience the ecstasy of dancing.

Abbey was born March 31, 1961, in Athol Memorial Hospital in Athol, Massachusetts, the daughter of Charles S. Plotkin and the late Natalie (Steinberg) Plotkin. She attended public elementary and middle schools in Athol and received her high school education from the Northfield-Mount Hermon School in Gill, Massachusetts, graduating in 1979. Her studies included a semester in Israel and one in France, where she studied Hebrew and French, respectively. She graduated from Emory University in Atlanta, Georgia, receiving a Bachelor of Arts degree in 1983. While in Atlanta, she formed a dance group called the Cracker Jacks.

Abbey took tap dancing lessons when she was very young, developed an interest in hip-hop, and quickly fell in love with salsa upon moving to New York City, where she frequently attended salsa dance events. In her early New York days, her friend Edmee Valentin and family embraced her.

Abbey founded Mambo Mamas, a female dance troupe that had an impact on the salsa scene. "Big Women," as she dubbed herself and others, were considered incapable of the fast moves and sometimes were not welcomed, but the Mambo Mamas proved otherwise.

She worked as a dance instructor in salsa, mambo, and line dancing. She was employed by the Arthur Murray Dance Studio as well as by senior centers, often arranging for her students to perform at various functions, including parades and celebrations. She loved living in New York City and essentially was a big-city girl from a small rural town.

Friends tell how Abbey changed many people's lives because of her example. She arrived in New York at a time when the AIDS crisis was devastating the gay community, and Abbey became especially close friends with a gay man named Manny, who was also active in the dance scene, but she was soon mourning his death from the disease.

She loved all dance, not just salsa, but that was her favorite. "On the two! On the two!" she would always say, a reference to where the beat should be. She traveled to salsa conventions in Italy and elsewhere, becoming well-known in the international dance community. Her friends from her days in Athol and beyond noted "she had touched so many lives through her passion for dance, culture, social justice issues, and LGBTQ rights."

Abbey's friend Edwin Rivera was one of the last people to talk to Abbey when she was hospitalized with heart failure. In a Facebook post, he writes,

> I felt your fear over the phone. Not fear of passing, but fear of not being able to dance with us again. Even in our last conversation, you were thinking about the dance community. "Edwin, I hope I get to dance with everyone again" were your last words to me. You were a gift from God to us, a trailblazer for the community. You did not see race, color, size, nor sexual orientation. You just danced inspired and brought so many of us together. You were a pioneer! These traits of yours definitely passed on to me, and I will forever be grateful to you.

My Strange Aunt Sylvia
2020

I wrote the following for family members
and sent it to them by email.
I also decided to include it in *From the Octagon*.

William Shakespeare wrote the song, "Who Is Silvia? What Is She?" for his comedy, *Two Gentlemen of Verona*.

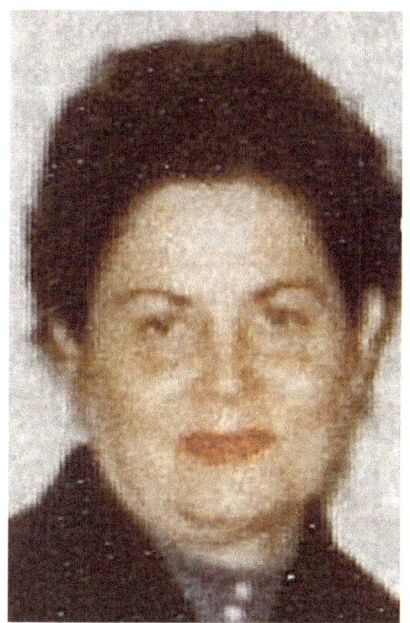

Sylvia Goldfarb
photo by Paul Laven

Who is Silvia? What is she,
That all our swains commend her?
Holy, fair, and wise is she,
The heaven such grace did lend her,
That she might admired be.

Is she kind as she is fair?
For beauty lives with kindness.
Love doth to her eyes repair,
To help him of his blindness—
And, being helped, inhabits there.

Then to Silvia, let us sing,
That Silvia is excelling;
She excels each mortal thing
Upon the dull earth dwelling.
To her let us garlands bring.

Today, I'm writing about my Aunt Sylvia Goldfarb, born August 3, 1914 and died June 14, 1986. The motivation for my remembrance is a moment in a December

2020 Covid-19 Zoom memorial for Sylvia and my cousin Herman Goldfarb, MD. That moment was a comment made by Herman's granddaughter, Leah Pearse, seventeen years old at that time and a first-year nursing student. Leah told the participants that her choice of a career in health care was influenced by her awareness that other family members were healthcare professionals.

Leah Pearse (2002-2023) inspired Allen Young to write about Sylvia Goldfarb. A successful nursing student, Leah died in a freak accident while on vacation in Cancun, Mexico. Leah's family considers the photo, above, their favorite of her. Another chapter in *From the Octagon* features Leah's grandfather, Herman Goldfarb.
photo courtesy of Amy Goldfarb

Thinking about her comment later, I said to myself, "Leah, at her young age, is probably unaware of Sylvia, who was a registered nurse." And I made the decision to write down what I knew and anything else I could learn.

The first line of the song, "Who is Silvia. What is she?" made me think of my aunt when I first read that Shakespearean verse in my youth. I knew Sylvia was a nurse and a painter, but I also knew she was strange, viewed by many family members as difficult and complicated. Although she was consistently nice and loving to me in my childhood, I also witnessed anger and hostility that she'd sometimes express in her interaction with my mother (her sister) and my father.

I also learned early on, perhaps around 1950, that she had been diagnosed with paranoid-schizophrenia and that she was under the care of a psychiatrist. I saw the doctor's name on pill bottles when she visited or when I visited her in her mid-town Manhattan apartment. I now presume the bottles contained some sort of psychotropic medication. I asked several cousins old enough to know Sylvia to offer information and comments. I got the following from my cousin Stanley Goldfarb, MD, Leah's great uncle, via email:

> I was unaware that Sylvia suffered from schizophrenia. If so, she must have been treated with Thorazine or some other first-generation antipsychotic because she appeared under relatively good control. In fact, she was gainfully employed as a private duty nurse for a number of years, although considered by some family members to be somewhat "odd."

My mother, Rae Goldfarb Young, grew up in a crowded New York City apartment. She was one of nine children, five boys and four girls. One of the girls, Dora, died early in life from spinal meningitis. The surviving sisters, Sylvia and Anne, were very close to my mother all through her life. One story my mother told about Sylvia included praise for Sylvia's cleverness. "You see," my mother said, "we all liked getting massages when the three of us were in bed together, and Sylvia was always in the middle. So no matter what way we turned, Sylvia was always getting a massage from one of us."

My mother also had her own view of Sylvia's mental illness, blaming it on the carnage of World War II when Sylvia served as a nurse in the US Army. Among her experiences, my mother said, was taking care of basket cases, soldiers who lost all four limbs and were placed in baskets. The term basket case is heard nowadays, of course, and here's what an on-line dictionary says:

1. dated, informal + offensive: a person who has all four limbs amputated [originated in the US after World War One]

2. a person who is mentally incapacitated or worn out (as from nervous tension)...also : one that is not functioning well or is in a run-down condition—an economic basket case.

More from Stanley Goldfarb:

> I know she died in the mid to late sixties because I visited her when she was dying with metastatic breast cancer in the Manhattan Veterans Administration hospital. I know this time to be accurate because I left NYC in 1969 to do a post-doc in Madison, Wisconsin, which has been my home ever since.

Stanley's memory is at least partially incorrect, because Sylvia died in 1986, but maybe she had an earlier bout with cancer, was hospitalized, and then got well again. Sylvia relocated to Florida, where she died. Someone told me she was buried in Arlington National Cemetery, but my search for her there via the website was not successful. So, I don't know where she is buried.

Stanley added,

> I also recall that when I was much younger, Sylvia recuperated from plastic nose surgery for a week in our Bronx apartment. In fact she was very pretty (as were her two sisters, Rae and Anne).

I had never heard about Sylvia having plastic surgery. Maybe she did, and maybe she didn't. But I do remember that I was told that my Aunt Anne had it done. Anne, when she was in her twenties, performed off-Broadway in left-wing theater and was apparently self-conscious about her looks.

Nose jobs, as they are commonly called (rhinoplasty is the technical term), have been a popular form of plastic surgery for women of varied ethnic backgrounds, especially Jews, who want to fit the Anglo-Saxon norm, which means bump on the bridge of the nose needs to be cut away.

Anne compelled her daughter Cora to have a nose job, too, when she was only fourteen, and years later, I heard several family members express shock and dismay about it. They pointed out that it was psychologically harmful to a teenage girl to essentially say, "You cannot be beautiful the way you are. You need surgery." The following 2001 article in a major medical journal is worth reading for more details about "the Jewish nose": jamanetwork.com/journals/jama/fullarticle/1844290.

When Sylvia was discharged from the military after World War II, she worked as a nurse in both hospital settings and private duty. When I was a student at Columbia College from 1958 to 1962, Sylvia was living in a rather new Park West Village apartment in Upper Manhattan not far from the Columbia campus.

I'd visit her for dinner on occasion. It was a short bus ride, and I think I just liked the connection with family that those visits offered, but I don't remember much about our conversations. Later, she left her Manhattan home and moved to an apartment in Co-Op City in the Bronx, where I visited her occasionally.

Expressing a viewpoint that I later found was rather common among nurses, she told me things about her work in a hospital. Mostly, she made comments about the doctors whom she disrespected for their lack of skill and/or their male chauvinism, or she commented about how doctors were disrespectful to nurses in general, which made her angry.

My best memories of Sylvia are from the time when I was from about ten to perhaps thirteen, when I visited her in the city on family trips to see my grandparents in Brooklyn. Though I was quite young, I was capable of riding the subway, and my parents thought that was okay.

Today, parental fear often stops children from having that level of freedom. Sylvia took me to the American Museum of Natural History with its Hayden Planetarium and to Ringling Brothers and Barnum & Bailey Circus. The strange thing is that I have no memory of her taking me to art museums!

I remember her apartment on West Fifty-Seventh Street in Manhattan with a long, narrow corridor barely passable because of many canvases of paintings, finished and unfinished, that she worked on. There were usually one or more easels set up with canvases—works in progress—and there was something appealing to me about the strong smell of oil paint.

Sylvia's identity as an artist was important to her and to me in my early years and later. Her style of painting varied. I remember a few canvases, but I don't know where they are. There was a small picture of a cat, copies of some Frans Hals paintings, and a portrait of Sylvia's father, my Grandfather Reuben Goldfarb. I also remember a large canvas depicting a candelabra with eight burning candles and one candle with no flame, representing the eight living children of Reuben and Eva Goldfarb and the one daughter, Dora, who died at a young age.

Sylvia was a student for many years at the Art Students League in Manhattan, and I was able to obtain a copy of her registration card from the school's archivist. It shows a variety of classes she took in the 1940s, 1950s, 1960s, and into 1970. The archivist told me it was likely she participated in the showing of students' paintings, but there is no documentation of that or of any individual exhibit.

She also studied sculpture and one piece that is extant, in my sister's possession, is a small table-top statue of three women, perhaps based on the three sisters (Sylvia, Anne, and Rae).

About a dozen or more of Sylvia's paintings were stored in an old chicken coop at a neighboring farm in the hamlet of Glen Wild, where I spent my childhood, and when I became aware of that, I took a look and decided they needed a home. Some were too large to put in a car, and they are surely lost forever.

I took those that could fit in a car and brought them to a family Passover dinner to see if family members would take them. Only one attendee, Lisa Goldfarb, took a painting, and it hangs in her home in Arlington, Massachusetts. It is a semi-abstract image of a vase of flowers. I took the rest of the paintings and placed them at an auction house in Deerfield, Massachusetts, where all of them sold in a single lot for about twenty-five dollars total. I kept the money.

Cousin Lisa recalled only that Sylvia had a strong voice, and she remembered stories she was told about Sylvia—both relating to her strangeness. Here is Lisa's email to me about those tales:

> 1. She had a cosmic ray collector on her roof. I have no clue where I heard that!
>
> 2. She was with a dying patient, holding her hand when she died. At the moment of death she felt the woman's soul leave her body and enter Sylvia via her vagina!! Myth? Urban legend? Those things stuck in my brain.

My sister Diane shared one of her most vivid memories. She said Sylvia told her, "I'm more your mother than your mother" and then went on to say that, when our mother was pregnant with Diane four years after I was born, she was contemplating abortion because she didn't want another child, but Sylvia talked her out of it.

At some point, I became obsessed with the idea that Sylvia might be a lesbian. While she was good-looking, she exuded a kind of unfeminine toughness. In gay parlance, she seemed rather butch. She never married, though one time, perhaps around 1950 when she was in her thirties, she visited our home with a man named Barry who was presented as her boyfriend. I remember him being quite homely, but what also makes him memorable was the fact that he was an electronics buff when television was first becoming popular. He introduced our family to television, and we thus acquired television much earlier than most of the people I knew at the time.

Sylvia once told me that when she was young, she dressed as a boy and hitchhiked all the way from New York to California. My cousin Michele Goldfarb told me that her mother, Goldie, my Uncle Ralph's second wife, used to be friendly with Sylvia, and when they were seen together, some people thought they were lesbians. I concluded that was because of Sylvia's affect and appearance. In today's lingo about gender, she might be considered gender fluid or nonbinary.

A very strange thing happened when I became involved in the gay liberation movement and started coming out to family members. Only one of my many aunts and uncles had a negative reaction—yes, it was Sylvia. She was very disapproving and told me so. I didn't really let it bother me, however.

Like several of her siblings, Sylvia leaned to the left in politics, but I don't believe she attended meetings or got involved with the intensity that my parents did. She used feminist and leftist turns of phrases. She once commented to me that she didn't like it when she was asked to give her race when filling out a form or questionnaire. "I just enter 'human race,'" she declared.

Just a few years before my coming out, Sylvia included me in her will as one of two beneficiaries. She named me and my cousin Sandra Goldfarb because of all the nieces and nephews, Sandra and I were the only unmarried ones. However, after I came out, Sylvia took me out of her will and replaced me with Cora Laven, Aunt Anne's daughter. I'm quite certain she chose Cora because Anne influenced her to make that choice. Sylvia was ill, and Anne was an attentive caretaker while my mother refused to play that role, so I just let it go.

I lost out on an inheritance of approximately twenty-five thousand dollars, but I didn't feel resentment or anger. After all, I concluded, she was mentally ill, and maybe that was an anti-gay act that resulted from Sylvia's internalized homophobia—a political analysis that had become quite popular in gay circles.

I initially used the word crazy in a very casual and unscientific way while writing this remembrance of Aunt Sylvia, and then, after conversation with concerned friends, decided to not use that word. My friend Stacia Friedman commented:

> If anything, Sylvia deserves compassion. Her mental illness does not make her crazy. That is just a term that was used decades ago when mental illness was not understood to be a health issue. She sounds to me like an independent, creative, resourceful, caring individual who lived at a time when those qualities in a single woman were not valued.

Having written my remembrance of my aunt, I return to Shakespeare's question, "Who is Silvia?" I offer the best response I can. My Aunt Sylvia contributed to society as a nurse and as an artist. She was strange, but she loved me, and I loved her, too.

Places

A Visit to Provincetown
2011

Provincetown Town Hall
photo by Diane Keijzer

Provincetown, at the tip of Cape Cod, has long been a destination. Henry David Thoreau visited Provincetown and wrote about it in his 1865 book *Cape Cod*.

No, he didn't write a word about same-sex couples holding hands on Commercial Street, commonplace in P-town's contemporary scene. The famed naturalist wrote:

From the first high sand-hill, covered with beach-grass and bushes to its top, on the edge of the desert, we overlooked the shrubby hill and swamp country which surrounds Provincetown on the north, and protects it, in some measure. From the invading sand, notwithstanding the universal barrenness and the contiguity of the desert, I never saw an autumnal landscape so beautifully painted as this was. It was like the richest rug imaginable, spread over an uneven surface; no damask nor velvet, nor Tyrian dye or stuffs, nor the work of any loom, could ever match it.

I recently took the fast ferry at ninety minutes from Boston to Provincetown with my sister Diane Keijzer, visiting from Aruba, to enjoy a two-day sojourn in the unique and beautiful town.

Joining a longtime friend who owns a condo there, my sister and I walked around town, while looking at some of many interesting shops and galleries and spending much time appreciating the natural environment as well as the architecture and culture.

Most of Provincetown's acreage lies within the Cape Cod National Seashore, CCNS, which celebrated its fiftieth anniversary in 2011. In 1961, President John F. Kennedy signed the law creating CCNS, originally filed in the US Senate by him, a Democrat, and Massachusetts Republican Senator Leverett Saltonstall two years earlier. I maintain that protecting this gorgeous seashore for future generations is Kennedy's most important achievement.

The highlight of her visit, my sister said, was the hour we spent bouncing with Art's Dune Tours on sandy jeep roads on seashore land, specifically through the Peaked Hills Bars Historic District. That is the area I wrote about in my book, *Thalassa: One Week in a Provincetown Dune Shack*.

A professional photographer, my sister loved the landscape and Cape Cod light that has inspired many artists.

We also explored the Beech Forest area where a boardwalk and sandy trail take visitors around a pond. We watched some resident Canada geese and their goslings at the edge of a glistening pond with many lily pads not yet in bloom.

While Thoreau arrived there in the fall, walking all the way from Concord, Provincetown is most popular as a summer destination. The majority of property owners have graced their small homes and businesses with recent paint jobs and charming flower gardens. The highlight for me, as usual, was the beach, because I like to swim, even in water apparently too cold for most of the sun bathers we saw.

The fact that Provincetown has become a major destination for gay men and lesbians is well known. The Portuguese community, once the dominant force with its roots in the fishing industry but now smaller, celebrates its annual Portuguese festival. When we were there, flags of Portugal were strung across Commercial Street, the principal business artery.

Everyone is welcome in Provincetown whether their focus is shopping downtown, nightlife with a variety of entertainment from drag shows to serious theater, or natural areas.

The beaches are popular, of course, in sweltering summer heat, with Herring Cove providing calm and somewhat warmer water, while Race Point offers surf and ocean views.

Sailboats, whale-watching tour boats, and a few private yachts can be seen in the harbor and nearby waters.

Considering we were visiting just prior to the Portuguese holiday weekend, I was wise to avoid heavy traffic by choosing the fast ferry from Boston, a service offered by two different companies. There is also a traditional ferry with on-board entertainment and a lower fare, but it takes three hours, twice as long.

Arriving or departing by water is uplifting, as there are no high-rise condos as with so many seaside towns nowadays. It's a very fine New England moment when one views Provincetown with the Pilgrim Monument and newly renovated town hall as the most noticeable structures lit by the bright summer sun.

Published in *Athol Daily News*, July 7, 2011
Copyright © 2011 by Newspapers of Massachusetts, Inc.
Used with permission.

A Ten-Day Visit to Pennsylvania
2011

One place I have long wanted to visit is Fallingwater, the unique house designed by the great twentieth-century American architect Frank Lloyd Wright and built over a small river on forestland sixty-five miles from Pittsburgh.

Last week, I returned from a ten-day car trip with Fallingwater as the main attraction. My partner and I drove approximately fourteen hundred miles on a well-planned loop that took us to several interesting places in the Keystone State.

Good planning pays off with a combination of peace of mind (a rental car instead of mine), an approximate budget that you can stick to, known destinations, and reserved lodging. I obtained information from local Chambers of Commerce as well as from the state tourism office and chose activities that involved nature, architecture, art, and some personal connections.

The first stop was in Pike County, Pennsylvania, to visit New York friends who have a second home two hours from Manhattan. It was at Hemlock Farms, a gated community with more than three thousand homes in three townships governed by complex regulations that, among other things, minimize tree cutting.

For insights into that kind of real estate arrangement—not common at all in New England but increasingly popular elsewhere—go to the Hemlock Farms website, hfca.com.

We then drove to Wellsboro to bicycle on the Pine Creek Trail through a narrow valley dubbed "the Grand Canyon of Pennsylvania" where fall foliage was excellent. For only thirty-two dollars per person, we rented bikes to pedal a seventeen-mile section of the scenic and well-maintained trail and were provided with a ride back to our starting point. Our leisurely bike ride included a good view of a bald eagle perched in a riverside tree, a picnic area we quickly left because heavy black walnut pods fell from the trees, and a hike along a dramatic waterfall.

With good marketing and adequate investment, I think the North Quabbin could support a small business like Pine Creek Outfitters, pinecrk.com, whose customers include hikers, bikers, paddlers, hunters, and fishermen. If not for them, we would probably have overlooked the beautiful area called Pennsylvania Wilds.

Next stop was Oil City in the region where America's petroleum industry got started in the mid nineteenth century. Located at the confluence of the Allegheny River and Oil Creek in the foothills of the Allegheny

Victorian House in Oil City, Pennsylvania
photo by David Malin

Mountains, the town has elaborate Victorian houses built when the embryonic oil business was making some people rich.

A friend had introduced us to artist George Cooley, formerly of Westboro, Massachusetts, who along with his wife, Nancy, generously offered us a full tour of their home featuring well-preserved hand-carved woodworking. We then spent an additional hour ambling through the neighborhood aided by a walking-tour pamphlet, as the region's promoters recognize the value of the region's high-quality Victoriana.

In an economic decline, the town attempted revitalization through promotion of the arts. Program coordinator Joann Wheeler gave us a tour of the National Transit Art Studios—formerly local headquarters for Standard Oil—and told us about an intriguing artist relocation program with information at artsoilcity.com.

A two-hour drive took us to Pittsburgh, where we visited the Frick Art and Historical Center and the Andy Warhol Museum. We rode up to a nice vista on the Duquesne Incline, a restored 1877 cable car, and had lunch in the Grand Concourse, a restaurant set in the stone, wood, and stained-glass splendor of the 1901 Pittsburgh & Lake Erie Railroad terminal.

Fallingwater, erected in the 1930s and open to the public since the 1960s, did not disappoint. The in-depth two-hour tour, wisely reserved months in advance, featured an articulate docent who taught us a lot about Wright's design. She revealed the dynamic between the architect and his wealthy but adventurous clients, the Edgar Kaufmann family, owners of Pittsburgh's largest department store. Partly because I live in a house

Fallingwater, the Frank Lloyd Wright masterpiece
photo by David Malin

also designed to emphasize the beauty of nature, I found being there an emotional experience as well as aesthetically pleasing.

Our next stop was Hawk Mountain Sanctuary, hawkmountain.org, in Kempton, where we hiked an easy trail to watch migrating hawks. We saw one kestrel, one turkey vulture and hundreds of other birdwatchers, but the view of the sun-drenched Kittaninny Range valley below made it worthwhile. The nature preserve was on my itinerary because my neighbor, Holyoke Community College history professor Diane Beers, taught me about Rosalie Edge's decision in the 1930s to conserve the land and stop senseless killing of raptors.

Before returning home, we spent some time in New York City where we satisfied our curiosity with a brief visit to Occupy Wall Street— there, we found not a bunch of lazy or wild-eyed extremists, as some have suggested, but calm, serious people striving for economic justice.

Published in *Athol Daily News*, October 27, 2011
Copyright © 2011 by Newspapers of Massachusetts, Inc.
Used with permission.

Monkeys, Birds, Beaches, People, and Planes:
A Trip to Costa Rica
2011

Although a car trip to Costa Rica is certainly possible and could be a great adventure, most visitors from the USA, including me, choose jet aircraft.

Winter weather causes havoc occasionally with air travel, and that's what happened to me. Havoc may be too strong a term, but snow caused a delay in my flight from Boston to Miami, so I missed my connection (by three minutes!), and had to wait five hours for the next flight to San José, the capital of Costa Rica.

Later, after I filed a complaint with American Airlines (why couldn't they have held up my connecting flight for five or ten minutes?), I received a five-star email offering elaborate explanations but no compensation.

Excellent guidebooks are available, packed with information about the Central American tourist paradise, so what's appropriate here are just a few of my personal highlights. I was traveling solo, so I focus in part on people I met.

On my very first day, whitewater rafting on the Pacuare River, including Class 3 and 4 rapids, was the exhilarating adventure I expected. At age sixty-nine, I was amused to find that almost everyone in our group of about thirty paddlers on five rafts were in their twenties and thirties. A guide told me that there are often older paddlers, so I can't be too smug about it.

The worst part of the rafting was listening to the guide's instructions about what to do if the raft tipped over or if any of us fell into the roiling water. It included mention of past incidents involving a variety of injuries.

The best part was having fun paddling hard, as well as relaxing, with a congenial group and a friendly young guide named Abel, whose expertise kept us all safe. My fellow paddlers included three students working on PhDs at Harvard's Kennedy School of Government, one of them a bright Swedish Oxford grad, Nils Hagerdal, who I half-seriously suggested might become that nation's next prime minister.

We spent four hours on the river covering about eighteen miles, all of it thorough pristine lush green jungle with waterfalls occasionally cascading into the river. The fee of ninety dollars included several hours of transportation as well as a delicious riverside lunch assembled by the guides.

Next was the remote Corcovado Tent Camp at the edge of Drake Bay on the Osa Peninsula in southern Costa Rica. My time there included swimming in the warm Pacific and a nature hike with an expert guide in Corcovado National Park. We saw two kinds of monkeys, a three-toed sloth, wild pigs called peccaries, raccoon-like coatis, crocodiles, lizards, and many birds. The guide had a spotting scope that helped us get a close-up look, and I also appreciated using the binoculars of a married couple, both doctors and expert birders, from Denman Island, British Columbia, Canada.

Among the people I met at the tent camp were a beautiful American woman from Wisconsin, her Argentine husband who looked like Mexican actor Gael Garcia Bernal, and her elderly dad who hiked around with a cane despite sciatic pain.

I especially enjoyed the company of two middle-aged American buddies, traveling without their wives, who struck me at first as loud good old-boy types from the South, but I quickly learned they were very open-minded, environmentally aware veterans of the US military whose views had evolved over time. Meeting them was a major lesson—one I thought I did not need—about not jumping to conclusions about people.

The camp was founded and owned by a middle-aged man who came to Costa Rica from the United States to surf when he was in his teens. One of his personal guests was a twenty-two-year-old high school drop-out from Long Island, a self-made millionaire who told me with an odd mixture of pride and shame that he owned a software business in San José employing dozens of Costa Rican computer programmers at one-quarter the salary he would have to pay them in the USA.

My vacation ended with several days at a nice hotel in Manuel Antonio. The highlight there was a nature hike in the rather crowded national park led by Gamaliel Pina, a personal friend of Athol native Scott Pralinsky, who had helped plan my trip. Our group included several members of a gay volleyball team from Portland, Maine, and we saw more monkeys, birds, butterflies, lizards, and bats.

I had excellent food during my eight days—lots of fresh fish, vegetables, fruit, and the traditional rice and beans.

I recommend Costa Rica as a tourist destination with many things to see and do, including ziplining and hiking on a Costa Rican trail around Arenal Volcano in Arenal National Park in central Costa Rica. I will definitely consider going again.

Visitors to Costa Rica may zipline over forest canopies, seashores, and the habitat of native animals.
photo by Scott Pralinsky

One of Costa Rica's natural features, Arenal Volcano highlights Arenal National Park with many appealing hiking trails.
photo by Scott Pralinsky

Published in *Athol Daily News*, February 3, 2011
Copyright © 2011 by Newspapers of Massachusetts, Inc.
Used with permission.

Mead and Beneski: A Visit to Two Museums in Amherst
2013

Exactly three years ago, I wrote about an enjoyable visit to the Emily Dickinson Museum in Amherst. Several friends and I were accompanied at that time by Polly Longsworth of Royalston, a Dickinson expert and museum trustee.

Amherst College owns two other museums: the Mead Art Museum and the Beneski Museum of Natural History, both open to the public free of charge.

Clare Green of Warwick, longtime friend and retired elementary school teacher, planned our outing together after being shocked to find out that I had never been to either museum.

Art and history along with nature definitely interest to me, and enjoying any of them in the company of a good friend is even better. Clare's offer to treat me to a cappuccino and a pastry as a fitting end to our cultural outing made the day all the more appealing.

The Mead holds an extensive art collection that serves the education of students at the prestigious New England College. Included are American and European paintings, Mexican ceramics, Tibetan scroll paintings, an English paneled room, ancient Assyrian carvings, Russian avant-garde art, West African sculpture, and Japanese prints.

The work of the Hudson River School of landscape painting is especially appealing to me, and I saw works there by Asher Durand and Thomas Cole, among others.

The museum is named for its founder, William Rutherford Mead, Amherst College Class of 1867. He is the Mead in the famous architectural firm of McKim, Mead & White, designer of the main buildings on the campus of Columbia University in New York City, where I was a student in the 1950s and 1960s.

One unusual aspect of the Mead is that the collection is in a fully illustrated and searchable online data base, and works currently in storage are available for visitors to see by appointment in a special study room.

Going to the Beneski Museum of Natural History caused me to have an epiphany about the phrase "natural history." It suddenly hit me that natural history is another way of saying history of nature, and just that simple rewording made me think differently about the experience.

When I was a child, my parents frequently traveled eighty-five miles from our chicken farm in the Catskills to New York City to visit family members, and my favorite destination on those visits was the American Museum of Natural History.

Like the big museum in New York, the Beneski's most dramatic items on display, whether to the eyes of a child or an adult, are fossilized dinosaurs. The Beneski has several huge ones as well as smaller ones, all beautifully presented.

Last April, the museum acquired the skeleton of a dinosaur that roamed North America during the late Jurassic period about 150 to 145 million years ago.

That Dryosaurus altus is one of just two such skeletons in the world on display as a freestanding, three-dimensional mount.

Clare and I were fortunate to have an Amherst College senior, Mauro Diaz, who hails from Texas, as our volunteer guide. Mauro took us around the museum and explained many details. We admired a mural that depicts the Connecticut River Valley as it likely appeared in the days of Lake Hitchcock—the body of water created as glaciers melted, and named for Edward Hitchcock, who was an Amherst professor starting in 1825 and later the state geologist.

The museum's website states:
> Hitchcock had wide-ranging interests, a keen sense of scientific investigation and the dynamic energy to execute numerous scientific investigations and ensuing publications. He also encouraged alumni to send back scientific specimens from all over the world and himself collected geologic and fossil specimens from local sites. One of these collections, the Hitchcock Ichnology Collection (ichnology is the study of tracks and traces), today continues to be the largest fossil track collection in the world and one of the most studied.

With a fifteen-million-dollar pledge in 2008, the principal benefactors of the building, were Ted, Class of 1978, and Laurie Beneski of Texas.

The museum's mission includes
> preserving and interpreting the physical evidence of the geological history of the Earth, the evolutionary history of its inhabitants, and the processes that have shaped both through time.

We should all be grateful for such endeavors in a time when religious fundamentalism threatens our nation's education system by rejecting well-established scientific evidence in favor of Bible text.

Chuck Longsworth of Royalston, Amherst College Class of 1951, president of Colonial Williamsburg from 1977 to 1994, and former chair of the college's board of trustees, emphasized Hitchcock's importance and stated that

> Amherst students are imbued with a sense of historical significance of their surroundings as they understand that the college is placed in the midst of glorious geologic evolution and they know about the fossil footprints found nearby in the valley.

The website amherst.edu/museums has lots of information about the Mead and the Beneski, including helpful details such as evening visiting hours.

Published in *Athol Daily News*, Dec. 5, 2013
Copyright © 2013 by Newspapers of Massachusetts, Inc.
Used with permission.

Creating a Meadow to Encourage Biodiversity
2016

A four-acre patch of land in Royalston, once dense forest, has been gradually and consciously converted into an expansive meadow to encourage biodiversity—that is, making it a home for a maximum number of different species.

Gerald Marcanio and Rob Jalbert, residents of the Peak House at Butterworth Farm on Butterworth Road, work hard to maintain their meadow—and they enjoy its rewards including open space, a large view of

Gerald Marcanio, left, with Rob Jalbert and their dogs
photo courtesy of Gerald Marcanio

the sky, and the opportunity to learn about, observe, and appreciate the many living things that inhabit or use the meadow.

It all started in the late 1980s when the late Bob Gravley, who built Peak House in 1974 with Steven McCarty, was ill and mostly housebound. He expressed a desire for the dense forest to be dramatically thinned so he could enjoy more of a view. A professional logger, Ted Hutchinson of Petersham, came and took out truckloads of timber.

Bob died in March of 1990, and for about fifteen years, the meadow concept was put on hold as the forest began to grow back. Following the guidelines of the National Wildlife Federation, Jerry and Rob then set their sights on creating and maintaining a meadow for support of optimum wildlife habitat.

Rob called upon his knowledge obtained from owning a modest landscaping business in the Boston area called Gardens, Etc., and he also went to classes in Brattleboro to become a master gardener. Two land-clearing specialists with machinery, David Lockesmith of Petersham and Bruce Scherer of Orange, worked on the project. Hundreds of saplings were cut along with some large trees not previously taken. Only high bush blueberry bushes and a memorial maple tree planted for Bob Gravley remained standing. That tree continues to grow and stands out nicely, and the berries are harvested to the extent that birds don't get them first.

They rented a stump grinder to get rid of about thirty stumps. From that point on, ordinary brush trimmers and lawn mowers were utilized. Jerry and

Rob dug up little saplings when they sprouted and mowed segments on a staggered schedule. "We don't mow the same area every year," Rob explained, and that maximizes diversity. Some areas get mowed every second or third year. Pathways are maintained with more frequent mowing, and in the pathways, one sees mostly grass— clear evidence that biodiversity occurs when varied amounts of growth are allowed.

Trailing Arbutus, left, the Massachusetts state flower, appears among the first flowers of spring followed in July by Wood Lily.

photos by Jerry Marcanio

The first flower of spring is trailing arbutus or mayflower, the state flower. The showiest wildflower that emerges is the wood lily with its bright reddish-orange petals. Every July, Rob and Jerry as well as neighbors and visitors anticipate its arrival. We enjoy wandering through the meadow observing various plants with their array of foliage, blossoms (many of them very small), and seed stalks and pods.

There are tiny wild strawberries but also some larger ones, hybridized with some cultivated strawberries from past gardens.

Other plants of interest include shin leaf, sweet fern, milkweed (important for monarch butterflies), boneset, Joe Pye weed, butterfly weed with its orange flowers, daisies, two kinds of asters, ten varieties of goldenrod, blue flag iris, smooth foxglove, blue beaded lilies, lady slippers, blue-eyed grass, partridgeberry, hops, clover, fleabane, mullein, orange hawkweed, and more. Edible fungi that can be picked and cooked are parasol mushroom, old man of the woods, and red russula.

Jerry, a skilled carpenter, built a half-dozen bird boxes carefully located near the edge of the meadow, and they have attracted nesting bluebirds, tree swallows, and black-capped chickadees, the state bird. The birds customarily nest in tree cavities. Bluebirds and chickadees ground feed both insects and seed during summer. Tree swallows get most of their food on the fly, and thus, another plus for the meadow is reduced mosquito population. Other birds often seen are cedar waxwings that like to eat berries and several varieties of woodpeckers.

Three Audubon Society field guides—one each for flowers, birds, and mushrooms—help Jerry and Rob to identify and learn details about the ever-growing number of species they observe. Some invasive species are a problem, and they are removed once they are discovered. They include purple loosestrife and European buckthorn.

The meadow provides a good place for a bonfire and improves the view of the sky. Rob and Jerry cut firewood to heat their home, gradually thinning the forest on the east side of the meadow, which helps expand a ridge view. The moon rises over that eastern ridge, and when full, the moon appears spectacularly large. When the meadow is snow-covered, the white surface is remarkable as it reflects the bright moonlight.

The rewards of the meadow just keep on coming, making all the hard work seem worthwhile. Rob and Jerry are my good friends and neighbors, and I don't have to do any of the work to enjoy what they've created—with the help of Mother Nature.

Published in *Athol Daily News*, January 7, 2016
Copyright © 2016 by Newspapers of Massachusetts, Inc.
Used with permission.

Small Monuments Found In Many Places
2018

Unexpected plaques and structures throughout the Quabbin region bring to mind events and people from the past. Some are poignant or thought-provoking, and it's fun to see them.

The Peace Statue in Memorial Park in the center of Orange on the north side of Millers River tops the list. The statue depicts a World War I doughboy soldier speaking presumably to a schoolboy with the haunting words, "It shall not be again."

Installed in 1934, the statue became the official Peace Statue of Massachusetts decades later under legislation filed by former State Senator Steve Brewer, D-Barre. The twelve-foot bronze sculpture by Joseph Pollia of New York attracted national attention when it was unveiled as a memorial to veterans of World War I. Orange citizens care for it lovingly and raised money to refurbish it in the 1990s.

Peace Statue, Orange
photo by Allen Young

In Hardwick, a boulder in Memorial Park honors veterans. A plaque installed on the boulder by Hardwick Historical Society proclaims that the Hardwick Fair, held annually and featuring the environment and agriculture, is the oldest continuous country fair in the United States. The plaque lists the many accomplishments of Brigadier General Timothy Ruggles (1711-1797), who established the fair in 1762.

plaque proclaiming Hardwick Fair oldest in the United States
photo by Allen Young

A plaque on Royalston's First Congregational Church recalls the region's most notable natural disaster, the hurricane of 1938. The Old Schoolhouse Memorial, a bronze tablet on a stone alongside Route 68 a quarter mile northwest of South Royalston village, is dedicated "to the memory of a group of village boys who here learned their lessons of patriotism and died for their country." The tablet lists eight names and depicts the school the boys attended prior to the Civil War.

Indeed, most area towns have war and veterans' memorials in prominent places, including Athol center with its veterans park, and there are other monuments in Athol that could be easily missed.

Athol History Trail signs serve to remind us of many past events, including Indian-settler conflict, the falling down of the Sentinel Elm, and the Underground Railroad that helped slaves escape to safety. A plaque on a rock in front of a house at 559 Petersham Road in Athol marks the birthplace of Lysander Spooner (1808-1887), a writer and activist.

Also in Athol, an old decorative small flower planter at the intersection of South Main and Mount Pleasant streets was a gift of the South Main Street Needle Workers, a women's organization, although the plaque that once identified it is gone. The planter originally served as a trough for watering horses.

The fountain installed in 1898 at the edge of the uptown common in Athol honors the memory of Ginery Twichell, a stagecoach driver, railroad magnate, and United States Congressman. The fountain stands near a former tavern, a frequent destination for Twichell and his team of horses pulling a stagecoach.

A fountain installed by members of an important reform movement in American history, the Women's Christian Temperance Union, WCTU, installed in Orange's Central Square in 1904, initially included drinking cups and a small basin below for dogs. The WCTU gained national prominence campaigning against the use of alcoholic beverages. Related to other popular reform movements and sometimes overly zealous, the WCTU blamed alcohol consumption for many of the nation's social ills.

A monument with a sculpture of a soldier holding a rifle serves as a World War I memorial in the center of Barre. It includes the names of those who served. Nearby is an 1866 monument featuring an eagle to honor soldiers from Barre who fought in the Civil War. In Hubbardston, the marble Civil War memorial also features an eagle.

A standing marble statue in Rutland commemorates those who served in the Civil War. The Civil War is remembered in another way on the walls of the main meeting room of Royalston town hall with names of men who died in the Civil War, citing the location of their death.

Civil War Monument, Barre
photo by Allen Young

A monument near the Pelham Historical Society building at the junction of Daniel Shays Highway and Amherst Road commemorates a late eighteenth-century encampment site of a portion of Shays's rebels against Massachusetts authority. The memorial commemorates General Benjamin Lincoln in big letters compared to those referring to Shays, who raised three thousand troops and routed the rebellion on February 4, 1787. It ends with the line, "Obedience to the law is true liberty."

A temporary alternative monument was brought to Petersham two hundred years later by two eastern Massachusetts schoolteachers who received permission from the Petersham Historical Society. The sign mentions General Lincoln in very small type compared with the type used for Shays, and its last line contrasts with the other plaque by saying, "True Liberty and Justice may require resistance to law."

A simple and eloquent monument in Shutesbury makes use of a millstone as holder for a bronze plaque installed on Memorial Day 1937 to commemorate Shutesbury soldiers in World War I.

Shutesbury World War I millstone monument
photo by Allen Young

A New Braintree road marker, erected during the 1930 Massachusetts Tercentenary, commemorates an event that occurred off the byway later called North Brookfield Road during the colonists' war with the Nipmuc Indians, named King Phillip's War. The marker says, "Edward Hutchinson's company seeking a parley with the Nipmucs was ambushed by Indians in 1675, and more than half were slain." While settlers experienced violence during the late seventeenth-century conflict during what amounts to essentially a land war, suffering of the Native Americans, then called savages, was as great or greater. White settlers, who saw themselves as civilized, decapitated Metacomet, the Indian leader called King Philip, and displayed his head in Plymouth on a pike.

Perhaps the oldest and saddest memorial is the Leonard Monument on Wendell Road, Warwick, just south of Moore's Pond. It commemorates a tragedy that took place in 1824 when James, the three-year-old son of Francis Leonard, was killed when he fell from a cart.

Belchertown Common hosts a number of war memorials—to soldiers in the Civil, Vietnam, and Middle East wars.

On the Phillipston common, the marker denotes the spot where a tree was planted in the 1930s by schoolchildren to celebrate the two hundredth anniversary of George Washington's birth. The tree is gone, but the plaque remembers it.

The website waymarking.com can lead curiosity seekers to many such markers.

published in *Uniquely Quabbin* magazine
January-April 2018

Two Unique Villages: Tully and North Leverett
2020

The word village conjures up a special place, small rather than large—a peaceful, cooperative, friendly, warm, and cozy community. A village likely has a cluster of well-kept homes, some grand, others modest—and probably a shop or a restaurant or maybe two, maybe an industry—or just as likely an empty factory building.

Most villages in New England have a geographical feature such as a hill or a river, a little park with a bandstand, a school or a place of worship, something old and something new—but more old than new. Without official recognition in Massachusetts as a municipality, a village may take its place as a neighborhood in a town or in a city.

Throughout the Quabbin region, residents experience sense of place and feel at home and connected to one another in many villages. Most of all, villages bring together caring people. Surely, that's what was meant by Hillary Clinton's famous book about education, *It Takes a Village*.

Dictionary.com defines a village as
a small community or group of houses in a rural area, larger than a hamlet and usually smaller than a town, and sometimes (as in parts of the US) incorporated as a municipality

The 351 towns and cities of Massachusetts have plenty of villages with no official or legal status. In our Commonwealth of Massachusetts, the concept of village remains undefined.

Leverett's North Leverett and Orange's Tully represent two of many villages in the Quabbin region.

Some 1,853 people live in Leverett, some of them in North Leverett, a historic mill village that is home to a portion of the town's population with the Sawmill River flowing through en route to the Connecticut River. By the mid nineteenth century, the village served as the town's industrial center producing lumber, shingles, and scythes. Industry declined in the early twentieth century, and some archaeological remains—including coke kilns used to make charcoal and the lumber mill built by Joseph Starrow—survive. Rattlesnake Gutter Trust preserves land in the area from development.

With a distinctly rural feel, North Leverett features predominantly residential buildings mainly Federal and Greek Revival in style, including the 1832 North Leverett Baptist Church. The Moore's Corner Church

North Leverett has a distinctly rural feel.
photo by Dale Monette

is in the Queen Anne style. The National Register of Historic Places listed the village as a historic district in 2014. The Leverett Village Co-op and New England Peace Pagoda, both established in the 1980s on their current sites, add a contemporary feel.

Paula Green, a resident of North Leverett for the past thirty-five years, moving from New Jersey, describes it

> as a wonderful place to live, with rural homes set deeply in the woods and room for a big garden. I like the people very much, a terrific mix. There are old timers who have been here for many generations, but most of us are outliers. I feel like we're all a bunch of refugees.

Paula and others find it appealing that the village is "close to Amherst, Northampton, and Greenfield, communities with some sophistication and interesting things to do." She participates with Hands Across the Hills, connecting people in Leverett with folks in rural Kentucky in order to facilitate dialogue and understanding.

Tully Mountain, elevation 1,163 feet, a popular hiking destination, rises above the village of Tully, called Tullyville on some maps. Tully Trail, Tully River (both east and west branches), and Tully Road go through the place, home to a substantial portion of Orange's 7,839 population. Tully Mountain, part of a state-owned wildlife management area, once had a stone quarry and a ski slope.

Jeff Cole, a resident of downtown Orange, spent his youth in Tully. His mother and maternal grandmother grew up there. He enthusiastically recalls

> the peacefulness of the village, the humming of the machines at the former Worrick Table Shop, but most of all,

Tully Pond in Orange reflects Tully Mountain at sunset.
photo by Mary Canning

there were plenty of kids to play baseball and ice hockey with. We used to clear a huge ice patch on Tully Pond and there was once a time when you could water ski on Tully Pond, but you had to know where stumps lurked!

The Tully City Council Club was founded in 1948 and met in a converted chicken coop until the building at present was erected and an addition was added to that in 1975. I remember Mayo Road and Packard Road were never plowed in the winter as the places were all seasonal then.

The Tully section of Orange nestles below Tully Mountain, upper right.
photo by Dale Monette

Memorial Day is a big day still in Tully for paying respect and visiting with family and friends at the fire station over coffee, donuts and lemonade. The new fire station replaced a station from about 1860 which still stands on Royalston Road.

On Tully Pond, the Athol Area YMCA operates Camp Selah, originally for kids from Worcester. People sometimes confuse Tully Pond with Tully Lake, a larger body of water located on Route 32 at the border of Athol and Royalston.

Locals know the Tully River, West Branch, as Tully Brook, once the site of Tully Brook Inn, a restaurant that closed in the 1970s. Gifford Memorial Conservation Area, a property of the Mount Grace Land Conservation Trust, contains an easy one-mile trail through forested land and along the Tully River.

Alex's Restaurant, long gone, sold Phillips 66 gasoline. A former mill building houses the Boiler Restaurant, formerly Tully's Mill Pond Restaurant founded by Stephen Thompson, called Tully Thompson, who grew up in the village. Other Tully businesses include Noel's Nursery and the Drew family's Porter Transportation.

Published in *Uniquely Quabbin* magazine
January-April 2020

Sleepy River Town in Brazil
1965

Conceição do Araguaia, Para, Brazil—When I stepped off the rickety DC-3 airliner that had just precariously landed on the grassy field, I left the modern world behind me. Isolation and inertia are a way of life in Conceição do Araguaia, here in the green middle of Brazil.

More than a dozen skinny barefoot boys clamored around the plane seeking to help the half-dozen passengers with their baggage. Isau Coelho Luz, an eager ten-year-old, seemed like the eldest boy present, and I chose him to help me with my small suitcase, which was almost as big as he.

In a way, Isau typified the village, a sleepy river town of some three thousand people, going nowhere as the broad Araguaia River flows northward into the Tocantins River and eventually into the wider Amazon delta.

Isau goes to school, where he is learning how to read, write, and figure numbers. Yet, he will find it hard to get an opportunity to do or be anything.

Isau, whose father died some years before, lives with his mother, grandmother, several aunts, and more than a dozen brothers, sisters, and cousins in a two-room house. A number of hammocks serve as sleeping quarters for the family, as is the custom in central and northern Brazil.

My own bed in the local boarding house is also a hammock, and the boarding house is little more than someone's home with a spare room and a few extra chairs at the table.

Six hundred houses comprise the village, about half of them with tile roofs and the rest thatched-roofed, mud-walled huts.

The people of Conceição do Araguaia do not have jobs in the normal sense of the term. Most farm some land in the village's environs, and many work as carpenters and masons. Some are employed on the many small riverboats that putt-putt their way up and down the river, selling goods from the cities in exchange for animal skins and durable crops.

On the edge of the village, three Karaja Indian families make their homes, barely mixing with the rest of the village.

Conceição do Araguaia was founded in 1896 by Fray Gil Vilanova, a French Dominican priest, and the Dominicans' influence has never waned. Only eighty people in the village have passed by Catholicism in favor of various Protestant religions.

Radio provides the major form of entertainment, and a few families have receivers strong enough to get programs from such distant cities as Rio de Janeiro and Sao Paulo.

The town has a mail and telegraph agency that has fallen into virtual disuse. The postmaster complains that he has not received his salary for months, the telegraph equipment is broken, and most people prefer to send their letters with those individuals who get out of the village by plane.

VASP airlines, one of Brazil's major domestic carriers, has flights in and out of the village four times a week as part of a three-thousand-mile flight between Goiania and Belem, making eight stops in between. Most of the passengers are traveling salesmen, missionaries, or owners of vast cattle ranches or plantations of Brazil nuts and mahogany.

The Brazilian Air Force also routes planes through Conceição do Araguaia, and according to Air Force regulations, passengers are carried free of charge whenever there is room.

Consequently, some residents of the village, including a few very poor people, have left the village and traveled long distances by plane for such purposes as visiting relatives.

But by far the majority of the village population does not leave. The riverboats are slow and uncomfortable, there are no roads in or near the village, and in any case, the only vehicle is an old truck run by the mayor's office.

Politics plays a small role in the life of the village, and at election time individual candidates declare themselves for one party or another. This is only temporary, however, and after election time the village is once again unified.

The village offers some strange vignettes. Every morning, early, a boy on a donkey goes from house to house. Two cans rest on either side of the beast. Each housewife goes up to the donkey, and the boy, never getting off its back, ladles out fresh milk.

A meat market sits at the water's edge. At 5 or 6 a.m., someone slaughters a cow or a pig, selling the meat at about one-fourth the price it might be in Rio de Janeiro.

One day, I asked a soldier too many questions, such as whether or not there was anyone in the local jail (there wasn't). He told his boss, and before long I found myself being questioned under suspicion of being a "subversive." I explained that I was merely curious and presented my passport, all of which satisfied the police chief, for he proceeded to issue me a visa for the municipality, misspelling both the words Conceição and Araguaia.

At 6 p.m., the sun falls from view, and it gets dark. Someone starts an engine, and the electricity goes on. A dozen townsmen gather on the corner of the only paved street, an incongruous strip of asphalt about 200 feet long, complete with a grassy mall and concrete benches. The men tell stories and joke with the visiting foreigner. At 9 o'clock, the lights go out. The stars burn in the sky; the village goes to sleep.

Published in the *Christian Science Monitor*
August 29, 1965

Having won scholarships, I lived for three years in South America.
I did some freelance writing,
including "Sleepy River Town in Brazil," above.

News

A Peek into the Massachusetts Legalized Cannabis Business
2020

"It's legal now! Finally!"

That's what people in many parts of the United States, as well as Canada and other nations, are saying, myself included.

To celebrate the legalization of marijuana in my state, Massachusetts, I recently used my journalist's credentials to obtain guided tours of two facilities related to the rapidly expanding and multi-million dollar industry. Both are located just a few miles from my home. One is MassGrow, a large cultivation enterprise, and the other is Silver Therapeutics, a small retail store, properly called a dispensary.

The main purpose of this article is to share with you what I experienced during the tours. But first, some relevant background.

Starting just about a century ago, fear-mongering, falsehoods, and distortions led to marijuana becoming illegal. Racism was also a factor because use of the herb was known to be more common among Blacks and Hispanics. Everyone interested in the history of marijuana should learn about a man named Harry Anslinger, one of the villains of the past century, who is the architecture of the anti-marijuana crusade.

The anti-marijuana crusade that ruined many lives has become more well-known and better understood in recent years. The mass incarceration of people of color, an issue discussed often these days, stems significantly from violation of drug laws, and those put behind bars have been mostly casual users, not big-time dealers or cartel chieftains.

Many who celebrate legalization are aging hippies like me. I was arrested in 1980 for growing pot in my vegetable garden, and fortunately, the consequences were minor (no jail time or criminal record—possibly a good example of my "white skin privilege"). My story is included in an entire chapter in my autobiography *Left, Gay, and Green: a writer's life*, reviewed in the *Rag Blog* by Jonah Raskin. Jonah's book *Marijuanaland* tells a more recent story about pot in Northern California.

The Rag is probably best known as the birthplace of the Fabulous Furry Freak Brothers, iconic 1960s comic characters created by Gilbert Shelton. The long-haired brothers were regulars in underground papers around the United States and beyond. One of the most enduring lines from the brothers is this: "Dope [pot] will get you through times of no money better than money will get you through times of no dope."

I mention it in part because legalization of marijuana and psychedelic drugs was a significant underground press theme back then along with opposing the Vietnam War and racism.

Athol, Massachusetts, population 11,500, a once prosperous mill town, was best known for two tool-making enterprises, L. S. Starrett Company and Union Twist Drill, UTD. A labor struggle in the mid 1980s led to closure of the UTD factory, then owned by Litton Industries, after decades of making an array of metal tools.

An early twentieth-century postcard depicts the Union Twist Drill company.

An energetic labor historian could write an excellent thesis on what happened in Athol over decades of union and non-union shops, but I digress!

The massive factory building that housed UTD was sold in 2018 for $1.2 million and became the site of MassGrow, the cultivation facility that I visited. The building was sold again two years later for $27 million. The purchaser was Innovative Industrial Properties, a San Diego real estate investment trust founded in 2016 as the first publicly traded firm on the New York Stock Exchange to provide real estate capital.

Clearly, cannabis has become really big business, and that is likely to continue on a global scale. The connection of cannabis to the capitalist system is an interesting topic that has been talked about for decades. I will share one relevant memory: there were very popular rumors, not substantiated, in the 1960s to the effect that the big tobacco companies were using the trademark system to grab well-known pot subculture names like Panama Red and Acapulco Gold.

As for the legal status change in Massachusetts, elected public officials are not the ones who made it happen. They no doubt felt it was too controversial. More than a decade ago, my friend Buddy Dyer and I were delegates to the Massachusetts State Democratic Convention in Worcester, and the two of us spent much of our energy approaching many politicians about legalizing marijuana with a focus on the taxation money the change would bring to help governments meet ever-growing needs. At that time, legalized casinos were being discussed, and we said that legalized pot would be a much better source of revenue. Each time, the politicians gave us no response except an embarrassed smile or chuckle, and that included a senator whom I knew had smoked pot when he was younger.

Activists placed marijuana legalization on the Massachusetts statewide ballot as referenda questions. In 2008, cannabis was decriminalized by a sixty-three-percent vote. In 2012, medical marijuana was legalized by sixty-percent vote, and in 2016, legalized recreational marijuana passed by fifty-four percent. Subsequently, the Massachusetts Cannabis Control Commission was formed by the legislature. Businesses then moved forward, but not very swiftly due to a variety of issues including finances, security, health, and zoning.

It struck me as almost laughable that the commission was spending more than a million dollars just to regulate a plant. The need to hire private security professionals and pay for elaborate laboratory testing added to the cost of the product, of course, and that's reasonable—but the bureaucratic aspects seem excessive.

At a zoning hearing I attended in Athol—remember, it's not a liberal college town but a rather conservative declining mill town—there was a fear factor palpable as members of the public commented. I took the microphone to call attention to that fearmongering. To make my point, I revealed my own history as someone using marijuana in moderation since my early twenties. I was the only one to speak openly in that way, though many people in the room were users.

Board members and other officials focused on the fiscal advantages, as pot sales could be taxed dormant real estate could be repurposed. So despite some whining, the town officials were welcoming, and no obstacles were placed in the way of pot businesses in the locale.

It became clear to me that those willing to invest in the pot business were risk-takers, because federal law still loomed as a danger. When I purchased items recently at the retail dispensary, I could not pay with a credit card because such cards are linked to large banks under the federal system. Customers pay cash or with a debit card.

Not only business but science became a big factor. Serious horticulture of pot was not something that I gave much thought to when I planted some seeds in my garden in the late 1970s. I picked off male flowers to promote seedless buds, sinsemilla, and I harvested buds along with leaves without much thought.

One thing I learned on my tour of MassGrow is that the leaves are now considered waste. In fact, they get mixed with kitty litter and disposed of as trash. Cultivation focuses on creating resin-filled buds—flower is the term that is used.

MassGrow cannabis ready to harvest
photo by Allen Young

From the moment I entered the MassGrow facility, I became aware of the role of serious science. There was a poster on the entrance wall about terpenes, a new word to me. They are aromatic compounds, considered relevant to cultivation of pot.

I was surprised when my tour guide, Kevin Rampelberg, instructed me to take off my shoes and put on special footwear and jacket. Later, when I told him that I was impressed by the overall neatness and order, he commented, "Cleanliness is fifty percent of the job."

Later, in a telephone interview with Andrea Cabral, chief executive officer of Ascend Massachusetts (of which MassGrow is an affiliate), she gave me an interesting insight into the way scientific research has changed the popular view of cannabis. So, for me, the goal of smoking pot is simply getting high. Today, when a customer goes into a dispensary to make a purchase, the salesperson asks, "What kind of experience are you looking for?" Just saying "getting high" is not enough. They ask, "Are you looking for mind-alteration, something body related, or maybe just help with sleeping?"

Andrea said it is a matter of users being more sophisticated. Once upon a time, there was bathtub gin and moonshine, she said, offering an analogy, but now there is craft beer and whisky and fine wines.

Andrea's background, by the way, indicates someone you might think of as unlikely to be in the pot business. She is an attorney and formerly served as the sheriff of Suffolk County—the City of Boston—and held the cabinet-level position, Massachusetts Secretary of Public Safety, under Governor Deval Patrick.

Genetics plays a big role in the sophisticated advancement of what I like to call "the sacred herb," and on my visit to MassGrow, I learned that they don't just plant any old seeds. They started with seeds from plants with specific genetic qualities, and now they don't even need seeds—they clone new plants from a mother plant with a name like Pre98 Bubba Kush.

Kevin took me from room to room to see plants ranging from little clones to four-feet tall and mature with substantial buds. He told me that there were currently 1,036 plants in a canopy of 2,072 square feet. Canopy is the term used by the cannabis control commission for cultivation area. While the old factory building space totals 360,000 square feet, MassGrow has focused its improvements on just 50,000 square feet. The plan is to invest $20 million in improvements and attract other marijuana-related businesses.

The plants are not grown in soil. There are no plastic flower pots such as the ones you'd see in a local greenhouse raising flower and vegetable plants for sale. The clones are placed in bundles of fabric filled with a sterile growth medium consisting of the ground-up fiber of coconut shells. Heat mats help promote root growth, while light-emitting diode, LED, lights help the rest of the plant.

No pesticides or fungicides are used. Elaborate tanks and pumps filter town water to purify it and nutritional salts are added—all part of an automatic irrigation system. Fans provide ventilation, and workers wear masks in accordance with COVID-19 prevention policies. I noticed mild aroma both inside and outside the factory building, but nothing offensive. Equipment at MassGrow has cost about five hundred thousand dollars so far, Kevin said.

Near the tanks containing fertilizer, I saw a huge pile of sacks with the name Jack's Salts on it, and the name of the company J.R. Peters in Allentown, Pennsylvania. I mused how pot cultivation in Athol is bringing revenue to Allentown, the third largest city in Pennsylvania. Family owned, J.R. Peters has roots going back to 1947, and its website proudly promotes its services to the cannabis industry along with to growers of all kinds of plants.

All of the MassGrow grow rooms are "feminized," Kevin explained, so searching for male plants—and removing them—is one of the necessary steps. Once mature after several months of growth, plants are dried, and then buds are removed by hand and by machine. As required by the state, samples are sent to outside labs for a variety of tests. Many buds are packaged for resale to retail dispensaries. Some are sold to other enterprises for processing. I saw workers putting buds into a small package containing 3.5 grams and labeled Banana Daddy as the variety and Ozone as the brand name.

MassGrow held a job fair to attract workers and, in a state that has one of the highest unemployment rates, an estimated five hundred people showed up. Starting pay is fifteen dollars an hour. Only thirty-five people are currently employed, but growth in the business is anticipated.

Silver Therapeutics is the name of the first retail marijuana establishment, or dispensary, to open for business in the region we call the North Quabbin. There are two others slated for opening in Athol, but their future is not clear. I met the co-owner of Silver Therapeutics, Brendan McKee, almost two years ago when work was being done on the site, a former law office just off the main intersection of Orange, population 7,500. I introduced myself and told him I was looking forward to the opening. We became Facebook friends and stayed in touch that way. He said the opening was delayed because the state commission is behind schedule.

Shortly after the grand opening, I made an appointment to meet Brendan at the store near the town's main intersection. The next building down is the historic Masonic Block, location of Orange District Court.

He gave me a tour of the dispensary, but first I had to show my ID to an employee at the entranceway. There were three other employees tending to long display cases in front of them and shelves behind them.

A few customers came into the store while I was there, but there were no long lines as happened with other dispensaries when they first opened in 2019.

Items on display included flowers (buds), pre-rolled joints, edibles, cartridges for vaping, tinctures, and paraphernalia such as pipes and bongs. I had some familiarity with these things, with the exception of tinctures, so I had to look that up later.

Brendan took me to the back where shelves were packed with stock and there was office space and an employee break room. When it was time to buy something, I said what I always say, "I just want to get high," and by that time I knew that I should ask for an item with a higher THC count. For more information on the difference between THC and CBD, the two sought-after compounds found in cannabis, I feel that WebMD is scientifically based and probably the most useful.

Though I like the ritual aspect of smoking, which takes me back to the good old days of the sixties and seventies, I had experimented with vaping in recent years when young people at a party offered me an opportunity. I thought it was okay, but I am not ready to spend money on a vaporizer and cartridges.

I wanted to do some more experimentation with edibles. Also, a friend just gave me a nice small bong. After discussing my desires with a staff member, I bought one hefty ready-rolled joint for fifteen dollars and a candy bar (one small square is the recommended dose) for thirty-four dollars. Both were enjoyable, but waiting for the edible to take effect is an inconvenience.

Of course, I know about legal homegrown—six plants per person per year—but doing it seriously takes time and energy. For decades, friends have shared homegrown and black market cannabis with me, and I don't consume all that much. Unlike some people I know, I have no problem paying a premium for a product produced with the benefits of science, hygiene, and state regulation.

Before I departed from Silver Therapeutics, I thanked the staff, and Brendan had some photos taken of the two of us. He wants to relocate from eastern Massachusetts to Orange to be closer to the store in Orange as well as the other Silver Therapeutics store in Williamstown, serving the northern Berkshires and southern Vermont.

I will end with a favorite story. A month after my 1980 arrest for growing pot was on the front page of the *Athol Daily News* and I had luckily kept my job as a reporter there, the editor called me over to his desk. He could have asked another reporter, but he chose me. He said, "The Athol Police Department is conducting a drug education program at the junior high school, so go over there and write a story."

Officer Bruce Boutall, who had a role in my arrest, was in the school gymnasium with Officer Al Torchia, and they had a display of items on a table. They held each item up and gave a little talk. When they held up a bong, they asked the students, "Do you know what this is?"

The response was immediate and loud from the vast majority in attendance. "It's a bong!" they exclaimed.

I laughed to myself, thinking that the cops needed to learn from the students, not vice versa.

previously published in the *Rag Blog*, theragblog.com

Workers Credit Union's Rich History Linked to Immigrants
2017

With a soft opening slated for December, the Workers Credit Union, WCU, will welcome members new and old to its newest branch, its sixteenth, in Athol's North Quabbin Commons. The moment is something to celebrate, especially in light of the WCU's fascinating history.

Founded in 1914 in Fitchburg, WCU was created and financed by first-generation Finnish-American immigrants with a fervent commitment to democratic socialism. The savings and loan institution, its devoted members filled with hope and optimism as they arrived in America, was a part of a growing cooperative movement.

In his 1981 book, *Blueberry God: The Education of a Finnish-American,* Reino Hannula writes,

The WCU of Fitchburg is the best example of a cooperative that was developed in a sheltered environment. This credit union, one of the first in Massachusetts, was organized by the board of directors of the Finnish socialist newspaper Raivaaja in 1914. The WCU was housed in the Raivaaja building on 48 Wallace Avenue for about 30 years. It was known among the first-generation Finns as the Raivaaja bank. The WCU prospered, even though it never hid its socialist affiliation, because it produced real savings for its members.

In fact, WCU went out of its way to identify itself as a socialist institution. As late as 1926, the credit union purchased an ad in the *Fifth Anniversary Review* published by the Young People's Socialist League of New England. That ad reads, as presented in the review:

> Workers Credit Union, Fitchburg, Mass. To our knowledge the only socialist savings institution in America. A purely cooperative organization. A deposit of $5.00 will open an account with us.

I note that the WCU is the most successful enterprise, which still exists, built by the first generation Finnish-Americans in the US and the largest institution of any kind built entirely by Finnish immigrant money.

Hannula added, "The Finnish American cooperatives were the most successful consumers cooperatives ever built in the US. There were in 1920 more than 150 Finnish coops whose combined annual business volume exceeded $5,000,000 in 1920 dollars."

Raivaaja's editor has long been Finnish-born Marita "Maba" Cauthen of Royalston, now with dual citizenship of Finland and the US, and I asked her to comment on the concept of socialism as seen by Finns. I also asked her about the name Raivaaja, which I had seen translated as "pioneer."

She noted that the title of editor is attached to her by the Raivaaja Foundation, which maintains a website, raivaaja.org, though there is no longer a printed paper. (By the way, for many years, the paper was printed at the *Athol Daily News*.)

Maba emailed me as follows:

> I have always felt that a better translation for Raivaaja is "trailblazer" rather than "pioneer." The idea behind the name is one who opens up new areas of thought. I

understand that the word pioneer can be used because it does not refer only to the land but the mind, too. Raivaaja's mission was to educate and enlighten its readers.

For Fitchburg area Finnish immigrants, socialism and the cooperative movement went hand in hand. They believed in democratic socialism, not in the state-run communism. In Finland, the state and the church had had a strong hold on their daily lives. Being in the US gave them freedoms they did not have in Finland when Finland was part of Russia. For the first time ever, they could fully make decisions about the course of their own lives.

When the late German author Günter Grass was asked why he was a social democrat, he said, "I'm a social democrat, because you cannot have socialism without democracy, and neither can you have democracy without socialism." I believe that is very much how the Finns here thought in 1914 and how many still feel today.

There will be seven employees at the new branch. One of them is Ryan Mailloux, who will be assistant branch manager. He is a member of the Orange Board of Selectmen and formerly worked at TD Bank.

WCU's executive vice-president and chief operating officer Sandra Sagehorn-Elliot said,

> The Athol branch is a full-service location. It will offer free WiFi for members, a drive-up ATM, a tech bar where members can test-drive our digital services, and a staff consisting of Universal Agents where each employee can assist with any need a member might have. We're excited about this because it means no hand-offs, the employee who helps you deposit a check is the same one who can help you apply for a loan.

The Workers' branches in Orange and Gardner are two of the busiest we have so last year we began looking for another site in this part of the state so we could better serve our members. The North Quabbin Commons is perfect for banking because people can get groceries, meet friends for a meal and pop into the credit union, all with only one trip in the car.

The WCU has about 4,500 members who live within five miles of the new branch, she noted. There is also a location at 32 New Athol Road in Orange.

Published in *Athol Daily News*, November 9, 2017
Copyright © 2017 by Newspapers of Massachusetts, Inc.
Used with permission.

A Deadly Disease Hits the North Quabbin: Heroin Addiction
2013

Steve Martin, MD, and Ruth Potee, MD
photo by Diane Keijzer

Ruth Potee, MD, and Stephen Martin, MD, a married couple, are like other primary care physicians treating patients with a variety of maladies, but what makes them unique is their commitment to combating "a deadly disease that destroys peoples' lives."

That disease, heroin addiction, is on the rise in the North Quabbin region as it is across the state and the nation.

Dr. Potee and Dr. Martin both have a strong connection to the North Quabbin, and Dr. Potee hopes to open an office here in the next few months to treat addicts and offer them hope for a brighter future. "The need is so critical," she said.

Dr. Potee, who grew up in Petersham, is a graduate of Mahar Regional School. Her father, Gale Potee, MD, practiced general medicine for many years in Palmer. Dr. Martin was a popular physician at the Desmond Callan Community Health Center in Orange from 2005 to 2007. When the clinic's administrator forced him out for personal reasons, many patients expressed outrage.

The couple resides in Northfield, and Dr. Potee works at the Valley Medical Group in Greenfield and Dr. Martin sees patients at the Barre Family Health Center. They both see many individuals from North Quabbin towns who are addicts and offer them treatment which may or may not be accepted.

An article in the Boston Globe recently focused on Dr. Potee's work with heroin addicts. The Globe report opened with this paragraph: Over the last two to three years, police and healthcare providers say they've watched a heroin epidemic take hold in rural, economically depressed areas of Western Massachusetts. Franklin County has been hit particularly hard.

The existence of the problem in the North Quabbin region is hardly news. Local organizations including North Quabbin Community Coalition and Hands Across North Quabbin have mentioned drug abuse as a significant local problem, but recognizing that plague is only the beginning.

All too often, the problem is swept under the rug, hidden from view. Handwringing provides no solution. Drug overdoses, like suicide, are public health issues. Obituaries almost always hide the cause of death when a drug overdose is to blame. That causes a "muted sense of urgency," Dr. Martin said, "as overdosing is the leading cause of accidental death in Massachusetts and nationally."

Heroin addiction nowadays often starts with the use of prescription drugs oxycontin and oxycodone, which transform the brain chemistry similarly to heroin. Whether created by a legitimate pharmaceutical company for use as anti-pain medicine or processed in illegal laboratories using the opium poppy grown in South America or Afghanistan, opiates offer people an opportunity "to create a feeling or get away from feelings," Dr. Martin said.

When "people want to escape their current lives," he said, opiates offer a pathway. Often starting with the prescription drugs, individuals discover pure heroin that has become cheaper, more pure, and readily available.

The physicians explained that it is easy to become addicted and very difficult to overcome it. Dr. Potee said, "It's like a high speed train from the first use to dependency to addiction." Dr. Martin recounted a saying he heard from an addict, "Once you are a pickle, you can't go back to being a cucumber."

The good news is there is a new remedy to addiction that has a success rate estimated by Dr. Potee at seventy percent, using a medicine approved by federal authorities called buprenorphine, trade name Suboxone. Drs. Martin and Potee are trained and licensed in the use of the drug, and they believe there are no other local physicians currently qualified.

Naloxone, a nasal spray, is another important drug that friends and relatives of addicts should know about. When an individual appears to be overdosing, administration of Naloxone can often be life-saving. Dr. Martin suggests that the medicine should be available in the home of any addict.

As a doctor, Dr. Potee said, getting someone off heroin is extremely difficult but equally rewarding, because it can mean returning that person from an abyss of hopelessness back to a useful life, holding down a job, and enjoying family and friends. To be successful, she pointed out, an individual must "want to be clean and sober." The tragedy is that not all addicts want to change, because the heroin high offers a powerful escape from dull and depressing lives.

Drug treatment is one thing. Improving our society so that people can have fulfilling productive lives is another.

High on heroin, "you can initially feel better than you've ever felt," Dr. Potee said, but if the person has the desire to escape addiction and return to a normal life, a skilled doctor with the right medicine can help.

Let's hope the plan to open an office locally comes to fruition very soon.

Published in *Athol Daily News*, August 1, 2013
Copyright © 2013 by Newspapers of Massachusetts, Inc.
Used with permission.
Update: The Opiod Task Force of Franklin County and the North Quabbin published a resource directory in March, 2025, listing the following places in Athol and Orange where professional help, including medication, is available for individuals stuggling with

addiction. They are Community Health Center of Franklin County, 110 New Athol Road, Orange; Clinical and Support Options, 2033 Main Street, Athol; and Clean Slate, 201 South Main Street, Athol.

Two Antique Ladies Visit an Antique House
2018

I obtained permission—with laughter all around—to use the term "antique ladies" here from two octogenarians, Betty Kimball and Helen Estabrooks, when I, age seventy-seven, drove them from North Orange to Petersham to see an iconic North Orange building on its new site in Petersham.

Our host in Petersham was Stephanie Selden, who transformed the old building into a comfortable residence on her ample Stony Lane Farm. Here is a perfect example of repurposing, a word often used for such a situation.

The building, which Betty and Helen saw just about every day over several decades in their little village of North Orange, was formerly the coach house or carriage barn of the Cheney House. Claire Chenausky of Orange, a friend of both Betty and Helen, told me that she was living with her family in the old house, then a rental property, when it burned down on January 28, 1967. The coach house was saved and acquired by the Community Church of North Orange and Tully.

Decades later, church members determined they could not afford to rehab the badly deteriorated building, so they planned to demolish it. Stephanie heard about that and decided to buy it. She hired a contractor to take it apart timber by timber in 2011, and it was then transported to her property in Petersham.

Stephanie offered the following account:

I was alerted that the carriage barn in North Orange was slated for demolition by friends in Orange who knew I wanted to build a barn at Stony Lane Farm. The barn was disassembled and moved in parts over a period of months in 2011. The structure was raised on this site in the summer and fall of 2011 by Roger Graves and Sons of Barre. The reconstruction of the timber frame to historic proportions that was the most challenging for Roger since there were no ID's on timbers or indication about their placement. The cupola was raised on Dec. 9, 2011. The interior was finished by Roger and crew in December 2014.

Ron DeJackome of Petersham gets full credit for landscape work including placement of original granite from the North Orange site. Gary Waid of Petersham laid up foundation brick here, using original bricks from the North Orange

Crane sets a new cupola in place on a building moved from North Orange to Petersham.

photo courtesy of Stephanie Selden

foundation. Doug Cameron of Petersham rebuilt the cupola, a replica of the original which had deteriorated too badly to be reused.

The original clapboards, exterior trim, window frames, distinctive corbels, sliding barn doors, slate roof, foundation brick, and foundation granite were all transported to Stephanie's land—quite an accomplishment. Thus, in addition to the original timbers, bones of the structure, the site in North Orange was littered with valuable architectural features "asking" to be reused.

Betty, Helen, and I were all impressed at how the old building had become a three-thousand-square-foot home, fully furnished, comfortable, and very attractive. Stephanie emphasized how much of the home is devoted to her nine grandchildren for their frequent visits. A bright red spiral staircase made of steel leads to the cupola, which must be fun for the kids. Stephanie found it on Craig's List, and it was moved to the site and inserted into the barn corkscrew-style through the hay loft door by Roger and crew on interior, with Ron DeJackome on exterior.

Betty enjoyed our outing immensely, thanking me and Stephanie and commenting,

It was wonderful. What a nice time! I loved the experience, and I did

Renovation complete with landscaping, the coach house appeals to adults and children.
photo courtesy of Stephanie Selden

love the house overall. I really liked Stephanie. The kitchen was great, and the dining-living. Upstairs, the renovation is wonderful, and yet I can see the old barn with all the pigeon poop! We used to store our attic treasures there for the church fairs. Glen Johnson and I were always going in and out, dealing with the attic treasures.

I feel wonderful that it was restored, and it looked beautiful having all the fields all around it, looking down toward the Quabbin.

Betty has a reputation for restoring old buildings and using authentic architectural features. She exclaimed, "I love that she used barn doors for the front entrance—very special in my mind, maintaining the purity of the late 1800s, when the building was built."

Helen said,

I've been telling everybody about our visit. I liked everything about it. I especially liked the fact that she made it into such a fun place, with the metal stairs going up to the cupola, and redoing the cupola. That was an extravagant thing to do, and the church had wanted to do it, but it was impossible. It was nice that she had swings for her grandchildren to enjoy. I noticed the homemade jam on the counter of the old antique kitchen. I loved the porch, wide and screened in. The open concept of the downstairs is very attractive but with a private bedroom placed in a former horse stall.

I'm pleased but not surprised that this little adventure I conceived of with my "antique ladies" was such a success, and I thank Stephanie for her creativity, preservation ethic, and hospitality.

Published in *Athol Daily News*, November 1, 2018
Copyright © 2018 by Newspapers of Massachusetts, Inc.
Used with permission.
Update: Helen Estabrooks died at age ninety-one in August of 2023.

Federal Anti-Lynching Law Passed At Last
2022

When I was a child, I saw a photograph of a lynching that took place somewhere in the Deep South. My parents had a variety of leftist books and periodicals in our home, and as a precocious child, I frequently perused them, and that's how I came to see this photograph.

In it, a black man was hanging by the neck from a rope while all around him white people stood on the ground and appeared to be entertained, as many of them were smiling. There were men, women, and children. I am curious by nature and didn't flinch from looking at it, but it was certainly a horrible thing to see. I never forgot it. From a young age, I knew that racism was wrong, as my parents helped me learn that important lesson in a nation where racism has been a powerful negative force.

I am now eighty years old, and when I hear something in the news, experiences from the past come into my consciousness–such as my viewing of that lynching photo. What I heard that provoked the memory was the fact that President Biden just signed a federal anti-lynching law.

The Death Penalty Information Center reported on the signing of the bill as follows:

After more than a century of efforts by civil rights leaders to make lynching a federal crime, President Joe Biden on March 29, 2022, signed into law historic anti-lynching legislation.

Flanked by the bill's sponsors, Vice President Kamala Harris, and family members of the late Ida B. Wells and Emmett Till in a ceremony on the White House lawn, Biden signed the Emmett Till Antilynching bill, officially denominating lynching a federal hate crime. The law allows for crimes–such as kidnappings, aggravated sexual abuse, or attempts to kill–to be prosecuted as lynchings in federal court when a conspiracy to commit a hate crime results in death or serious bodily injury. Individuals convicted of lynching face punishment of up to 30 years in prison.

"Lynching was pure terror to enforce the lie that not everyone belongs in America, not everyone is created equal," Biden said after signing the bill. Citing recent high-profile incidents of racist violence, he warned that racism remains "a persistent problem" across the United States.

Biden said,

From the bullets in the back of Ahmaud Arbery to countless other acts of violence–countless victims known and unknown–the same racial hatred that drove the mob to hang a noose brought that mob carrying torches out of the fields of Charlottesville just a few years go.

Racial hate isn't an old problem; it's a persistent problem. A persistent problem. And I know many of the civil rights leaders here know, and you heard me say it a hundred times: Hate never goes away; it only hides. It hides under the rocks. And given just a little bit of oxygen, it comes roaring back out, screaming. But what stops it is all of us, not a few. All of us have to stop it.

The bill is named for Emmett Till, a teenager from Chicago who was lynched in Mississippi in 1955. Till, who was fourteen at the time, was visiting relatives when a white woman accused him of whistling at her.

He was kidnapped, beaten, and brutally killed. His assailants threw his body, weighed down by a metal fan tied to his neck, into a river. Two men were charged with his murder but were acquitted by an all-white, all-male jury. At Till's funeral, his mother, Mami Till, insisted on an open casket to expose publicly the violence inflicted on her son.

Encyclopedia Britannica defines lynching as

> a form of violence in which a mob, under the pretext of administering justice without trial, executes a presumed offender, often after inflicting torture and corporal mutilation. The term "lynch law" refers to a self-constituted court that imposes sentence on a person without due process of law. Both terms are derived from the name of Charles Lynch (1736–96), a Virginia planter and justice of the peace who, during the American Revolution, headed an irregular court formed to punish loyalists.

There is more in *Wikipedia*.

One could say that lynching is a form of vigilante justice, and I don't like vigilante justice of any kind, causing me to reject narratives projecting it as a good thing. An example of this is a popular 1996 movie entitled *Sling Blade*, in which the likeable hero, played by Billy Bob Thornton, uses violence to end his mistreatment, and the viewer is supposed to welcome it. Presumably welcomed by the viewer, vigilante justice prevails in another movie, *In the Bedroom,* 2001, starring Tom Wilkinson and Sissy Spacek.

Signing of the federal anti-lynching law came around the same time as the release of a new book, *White Lies*. Author A.J. Baime tells the story of Walter White, a light-skinned Black man whose ancestors had been enslaved. For years, White risked his life investigating racial violence in the South, and he served as executive director of the National Association for the Advancement of Colored People, NAACP, from 1931 to 1955. Dave Davies of the National Public Radio show *Fresh Air* reviews the book.

I first learned about Walter White in the context of his efforts to have Congress pass an anti-lynching law in the 1930s. That history lesson came as I was reading *Eleanor Roosevelt: Volume Two, 1933-1938* by Blanche Weisen Cook, published a decade ago.

As first lady during the presidency of Franklin Delano Roosevelt, Eleanor was a politically astute and active woman who had a friendship with Walter White. She supported the NAACP's effort to have the United States adopt an anti-lynching law but could not convince her husband to support it. He needed the votes of southern Democrats, and he assumed (probably correctly) that his support for such a law would damage him politically. FDR served four terms as president of the US, and that was during a time when southern states were dominated by the Democratic Party.

Lynching in the "style" of the photograph I saw as a child has not occurred recently, as far as I know, but the concept of the noose as a racist symbol endures. MSNBC recently reported that "Nooses, which are associated with acts of lynching in the United States, are one of the prevailing symbols of hate, violence, and white supremacy."

Biden linked the new law to the shooting of Ahmaud Arbery, and since the *Rag Blog* is published in Texas, it is appropriate for me to also recall the case of the horrible and violent death of James Byrd Jr. as a lynching.

We don't have much to celebrate when it comes to action by the US Congress in 2022, but the passage of the anti-lynching law is a welcome exception. With so much bad news overwhelming us, let's spend a few minutes to appreciate good news. It won't end racism, but every little bit helps. That's what the word progressive implies, I believe.

previously published in the *Rag Blog*, theragblog.com

Millions React to the Beginning of the Trump Era
2017

I was one of millions of people around the world who reacted to the beginning of the era of Donald Trump as president of the United States of America by going into the streets. As previously mentioned in my *Athol Daily News* column, I attended a support rally in Greenfield related to the so-called Women's March in Washington, DC.

A significant number of people from the North Quabbin region went to Greenfield, where an estimated three thousand people held a variety of signs, wore pink pussy hats mocking Trump's vulgar comments about women, and felt good about taking a step in opposition to Trump's words and appointments. There were many multi-generational marchers. For example, Rice Flanders of Orange went to Washington with her son Gabriel and grandson Luke. Current and former residents of the North Quabbin who are among my Facebook friends went to marches in Boston, New York, Austin, and San Francisco.

What those people will do next is unclear, but there's talk of continued action and organizing. The sheer number of people who felt moved to take to the streets is itself a message.

However, it seems that Trump supporters and others who are neutral have little patience for the outpouring of opposition. Well, that's their right, but I don't see how they can ignore the historic outpouring of concern. Maybe it makes them feel better to focus on a few incidents of vandalism on Inauguration Day and on Madonna's unwise use of foul language and her childish thoughts of "blowing up" the White House. They also like to say that protestors are just a bunch of whiners and sore losers.

Carla Rabinowitz of Royalston offered the following response to that line of thinking:

> To me, the march was about a great deal more than women's rights. It was about the future of the American ideal. We were not "whining" because our candidate lost—we were declaring our intention to stand up and fight against whatever damage our new president will try to do to that ideal.
>
> We are terrified. Terrified by the outbreak of racist and anti-Semitic violence across the country—well over seven hundred hate crimes reported since the election, dozens of bomb threats against synagogues, and even Jewish daycare centers in the past week. We are terrified on behalf of the thirty-two million people who, according to the non-partisan Congressional Budget Office, will lose their health insurance if the Affordable Care Act is repealed.
>
> We are terrified by the prospect of forced registration of Muslims, an echo of one of the dark moments of twentieth-century America and of the incomparably greater darkness across the ocean. We are terrified by the reality that our new president neither understands nor respects the Bill of Rights and is ready to shred it at the first opportunity. We are terrified that he does not want to know the truth and lashes out at his own intelligence service when it tries to tell him. Most of all, we are terrified that he is ready to sell our country to its most dangerous, most aggressive adversary, to line his own pockets, because he

is in debt to its oligarchs or because he cannot resist the flattery of its dictator.

Lynn Kellner of Royalston said,

I went to the march in NYC. Some estimates were that there were four hundred thousand people. The march was so big, the police kept expanding the area from a few lanes to the width of the streets and finally to the sidewalks. Forty-Second Street was filled with marchers over the whole street and both sides of the sidewalks. The police were remarkably friendly, which was interesting. I was impressed with the number of issues that people were representing, and the wide range of ages, race, and so on represented.

Kim Marshall of Orange wrote on Facebook,

For those of you who haven't taken the time to understand what today's marches are about…We will fight for criminal justice reform, reproductive rights, immigrant rights, quality public education, LGBTQ rights, economic justice, environmental protection, disability rights, and health care for all. Just to name a few.

Don't even think about posting on my Facebook page that this is crying over the election. I believe in our democracy and the Electoral College has spoken. Trump is the President. Because when you dismiss someone who doesn't support the same things you do you attempt to silence that person. It's an act of bullying. I will not stand for it. Don't ever try to gaslight me. I will fight back. And that is fair warning.

Endorsing the Washington march—which he participated in—Congressman Jim McGovern, D-Massachusetts Second District, said,

It is important that we make clear to President Trump that we will not acquiesce in the face of policies that we deplore. Politics is not about rolling over, politics is about standing up and fighting for what you believe in.

Published in *Athol Daily News*, January 26, 2017
Copyright © 2017 by Newspapers of Massachusetts, Inc.
Used with permission.

Update: Trump completed one term and was defeated at the polls by Joe Biden in 2020, though Trump then led an insurrection based on the false claim that he (Trump) was the true winner. In November of 2024, voters once again had the opportunity to elect, or to reject, Donald Trump, and they returned him to the presidency. Widespread resistance is growing to Trump and his policies.

Views

Vermont Nuke Is Old. It's Time to Shut it Down
2010

From the tower atop Mount Grace in Warwick, there's a good view of the Vermont Yankee Nuclear Power Plant in Vernon, Vermont. You can see how close it is to us, and as problems at the plant become more serious, it's a matter of self-preservation that we—citizens and government—strive to have it shut down as soon as possible.

The current increase in calls for shutting down the plant is a direct response to the owner's request to allow it to operate for twenty more years after its current license expires in 2012.

Problems at the plant are frequent and complex, and even Vermont's Governor Jim Douglas, a pro-nuke Republican, has called for the plant's owner, Louisiana-based Entergy Corporation, to replace its top Vermont managers.

Last month, groundwater monitoring wells in two locations at the reactor, on the banks of the Connecticut River, were found to be contaminated at dangerous levels with the radioactive isotope tritium. It was revealed, during an investigation of the source, that underground pipes were involved—except that the company previously testified that no such pipes existed. Company officials apologized for the "misinformation," but the level of mistrust has risen sharply.

The spokesman for Vermont Yankee said,

> The existence of tritium in such low levels does not present a risk to public health or safety whatsoever. And there has been no elevated tritium level found in any drinking water well samples or in Connecticut River water.

William Irwin, radiological health chief for the Vermont Department of Health, said it was obvious that the tritium-tainted water was draining into the Connecticut River. He said the huge volume of river water was diluting the radioactive contamination to an immeasurable level, but he also announced that the state had increased its testing of wells in the area, particularly at the nearby Vernon Elementary School.

This sounds scary to me, as does the fact that the company provides all residents within ten miles of the facility (that includes part of Warwick, Massachusetts) with special emergency warning alarms in their homes and iodine pills to help prevent radiation sickness if ever there is a disaster.

Entergy Corporation is a Fortune 500 company that owns a dozen nukes in several states, primarily in the Southeast, and sells electricity to millions of residential and commercial customers. It's a huge enterprise with all sorts of problems. How can it possibly pay the proper amount of attention to the relatively small Vermont plant, where leaks and storage of radioactive waste are a constant concern?

Entergy has missed deadlines for installing emergency sirens at a plant it owns in New York, and it earned the lowest customer service ratings of any large utility in the South providing residential service. The firm is pursuing a complex financial deal to create a spin-off company that would own five of its nuclear plants, including

Vermont Yankee, and it is involved with three applications to the federal government to build new reactors.

The New England Coalition on Nuclear Pollution, an organization that opposes the nuke, is urging the Vermont Public Service Board, to act against Entergy. The Coalition points out that decommissioning the nuke and cleaning up the site are obviously going to cost more as a result of the tritium incident.

Massachusetts residents, including many of my friends and me, have joined their neighbors in Vermont and New Hampshire for a long time in calling for the closing of this nuke. The *Athol Daily News* published articles I wrote in the 1970s about participation of local residents in demonstrations at Vernon, and this newspaper is to be congratulated for remaining attentive to the nuclear issue, including articles about the continued anti-nuke efforts of area residents.

Published in *Athol Daily News*, February 4, 2010
Copyright © 2010 by Newspapers of Massachusetts, Inc.
Update: Following many demonstrations at the site of the plant, as well as continued negative news about its functioning, the Vernon nuke was shut down on December 29, 2014. Cleanup continues.

In Defense of Drag Queens
2023

Drag queens have recently become the target of right-wing politicians in several Republican-dominated states, and while I've never been a drag queen and have seen only a few drag shows, I feel moved to write something on the topic.

I'm a gay man with decades of experience in the gay community and a strong feminist consciousness, and I also like to think I have a healthy sense of humor and the ability to avoid stifling dogma.

Full disclosure: I have put on women's dresses a few times myself to participate in a party or because a friend coaxed me into it to prove I'm not "up tight." Back in the 1970s, when bearded men like me wore dresses, it was called "genderfuck." I also tried my mother's lipstick once—it tasted bad, and that was the end of that.

Author Allen Young in a dress
photo by Carl Miller

Before further commenting on drag queens in the news of the day, I want to call attention to *AJ and the Queen*, a relevant and entertaining TV show. While searching on Netflix for something to watch, my partner and I came upon a series starring RuPaul, certainly America's best-known drag queen.

RuPaul Andre Charles, 63, is an African-American gay man married to another man and best known for producing, hosting, and judging the reality competition series, *RuPaul's Drag Race*—and he's won many awards. Learn more about him at *Wikipedia*.

AJ and the Queen is a one-season show with ten episodes.

AJ is a ten-year-old girl runaway, Amber Jasmine, played by an actress named Izzy G., and the queen is Ruby Red, a character much like RuPaul himself. The series is about a road trip, with Ruby Red traveling to earn money in drag shows in various cities while AJ—sadly alienated from her mother, an addict and sex worker—hopes Ruby will deliver her to her grandfather in Texas.

Gender politics enters briefly in the series, as AJ is, at the outset, dressed as a boy. AJ tells Ruby Red that she has disguised herself as a boy "because boys have it easier," but Ruby reassures AJ that it's okay to be a girl—and she drops the disguise.

What I liked the most about the series is its insight into drag as an established aspect of modern gay male subculture, featuring all the elaborate costumes and wigs as well as the gay bars in cities large and small all over the USA that feature drag shows. The viewer gets to meet Ruby's friend, a costume designer having an affair with a gay police officer, as well as many drag queens in the various clubs.

There are some insights into the competitive and sometimes bitchy nature of the drag world as well as true respect for female entertainment icons such as Cher and Diana Ross.

The series is entertaining, but sometimes the dialogue gets a little preachy, and the confusing plot involves a pair of odd villains. One of them is a nasty woman with an eye patch, and the other is Ruby Red's former boyfriend, a grifter.

Let me be clear by stating that drag is not the same as transgender. Drag queens, possibly with some exceptions, are trans in the most transitory way—that is, they are men, almost always gay men, who impersonate women using elaborate costumes. They don't want to be women.

I was confident that I could define drag queen without help, but I decided to go to Google and ask, "What is a drag queen?" I got a very good answer with a referral to the *Wikipedia* page where it says:

> A drag queen is a person, usually male, who uses drag clothing and makeup to imitate and often exaggerate female gender signifiers and gender roles for entertainment purposes. Historically, drag queens have usually been gay men, and have been a part of gay culture.

That's a perfect definition, as far as I am concerned.

Here's another useful definition I found in *Wikipedia* of the word drag, showing a broader use of the term:

> The term drag refers to the performance of exaggerated femininity, masculinity, or other forms of gender expression, usually for entertainment purposes. Drag usually involves cross-dressing. A drag queen is someone (usually

male) who performs femininity and a drag king is someone (usually female) who performs masculinity. Performances often involve comedy, social satire, and at times political commentary. The term may be used as a noun as in the expression in drag or as an adjective as in drag show.

Ru Paul makes it quite clear in the series that carries his name that he is a gay man in the world of entertainment, not someone dissatisfied with being male and desirous of becoming female. And that is a fair way to describe most drag queens.

It can get complicated. There are heterosexual men who like to dress in women's clothes because it excites them (sexual arousal)—but they want to have sex with women, not with other men. Hundreds of such heterosexual men, sometimes called crossdressers or transvestites, gather with some gay transvestites annually for Fantasia Fair in October in Provincetown. The first such fair was held in 1975.

Drag has been around a long time and in various forms. The Jewel Box Revue, founded in 1939, was a troupe of so-called female impersonators, the term they used, who performed in many venues around the United States over several decades. The cast of the show, primarily gay men, dressed and performed very convincingly as women, and for the most part, they did not perform in gay venues but in nightclubs where the audiences were primarily heterosexual. My impression is that straight men were intrigued by those very attractive individuals who looked just like women but who, it was crystal clear, did not have vaginas. There was humor in that simple scenario.

Drag shows in gay bars essentially attract a gay male audience with perhaps some lesbians and straight people. Over decades, television and movies brought drag to a wide audience. Milton Berle, one of the biggest stars of TV in the 1950s, regularly appeared on the tube in drag. In 1949, Berle graced the cover of Newsweek magazine all dolled up like Carmen Miranda. Flip Wilson, a black comedian, developed a popular character named Geraldine. In the 1959 movie *Some Like it Hot*, two male musicians played by Tony Curtis and Jack Lemon witness a mob hit and flee the state disguised as women in an all-female band.

A struggling actor played by Dustin Hoffman cross-dressed for success in the 1982 movie, *Tootsie*. In more recent years, Tyler Perry created and played the part of Mabel "Madea" Simmons, a tough elderly woman, in several films. And let's not forget Les Ballets Trockadero de Monte Carlo, founded in 1974 by a group of trained ballet dancers for the purpose of presenting a playful, entertaining view of traditional, classical ballet in parody form. The all-male troupe members wear tutus and do ballerina steps, while the performers' off-stage sexual orientation is not an issue and not discussed. I saw them perform at the University of Massachusetts Fine Arts Center, and they are talented and entertaining.

For decades, all the cross-dressing in the media, as far as I could determine, was not controversial and not discussed in the political arena. It was just entertainment mostly seen as something to laugh at or at least to smile or chuckle at, not something to rant and rave against.

So, what happened? It seems to me that current anti-drag politics is an offshoot of the endeavor to deny any rights or freedom of choice to transgender individuals.

Laws restricting transgender people, passed in several states with more on the way, seem to be paving the way for action against drag queens.

Most politicians taking that path were already against same-sex marriage. Republicans, after all, have steadfastly opposed gay rights legislation in the US Congress for many years.

The idea that homosexuality is related to pedophilia—sex with children—has been floating around right-wing circles for decades. When Anita Bryant launched her anti-gay campaign in Florida in the 1970s, it was called Save Our Children. Lately, hateful right-wingers are accusing drag queens of "grooming" children for sex. A few years ago, drag queens in San Francisco launched something called *Drag Story Hour, DSH,* and it seems relevant to current events. Here's what it says on the *DSH* website:

> What is *Drag Story Hour*? It's just what it sounds like—storytellers using the art of drag to read books to kids in libraries, schools, and bookstores. *DSH* captures the imagination and play of the gender fluidity of childhood and gives kids glamorous, positive, and unabashedly queer role models. In spaces like this, kids are able to see people who defy rigid gender restrictions and imagine a world where everyone can be their authentic selves! *Drag Story Hour, DSH,* was created by Michelle Tea and RADAR Productions under the leadership of Julián Delgado Lopera and Virgie Tovar in San Francisco in 2015. It started out as drag queens reading stories to children in libraries and grew into a global phenomenon. *DSH* now offers literary and creative programming for kids and teens of all ages led by drag queens, kings, and all other royal beings. *DSH* is a national 501c3 non-profit with a global network of local organizations, each of which is independently managed and funded.

Drag queens reading stories to children is not sexual activity, but right-wingers suggested something illicit was going on.

Laws were passed in Texas and Florida and perhaps elsewhere restricting drag activities. In Florida, the legislature acted after Governor Ron DeSantis's administration filed a complaint against the Hyatt Regency Miami hotel for hosting a Drag Queen Christmas event in December 2022.

A portion of the population goes along with it, but there has been pushback. For example, a popular restaurant in Orlando that hosts drag brunches filed a lawsuit against DeSantis, claiming it lost business because of the signed law that has been widely interpreted by LGBTQ advocates as a crackdown on drag shows.

The owner of Hamburger Mary's Orlando says their First Amendment rights were violated when DeSantis signed a bill restricting attendance of children at certain performances, according to the lawsuit. The restaurant is asking the court to block the implementation of the law.

A statement posted on the restaurant's Facebook page reads: "

> This bill has nothing to do with children, and everything to do with the continued oppression of the LGBTQ+ community. Anytime our legislators want to demonize a group, they say they are coming for your children. In this case, creating a false narrative that drag queens are grooming and recruiting your children with no factual basis or history to back up these accusations AT ALL.

An acquaintance of mine recently posted a comment on Facebook indicating that anti-drag politics has become quite public. He writes:

> Last weekend, the family watched *The Birdcage*. Neither of the kids had seen it, and I always remembered liking it. And, it has a great cast with Robin Williams, Nathan Lane, Gene Hackman, and Dianne Wiest. Hank Azaria has a notable performance, too. The movie is now twenty-seven years old, and the story centers on a gay couple (Williams and Lane) that owns the most popular drag club in South Beach, Miami, Florida. Lane is the star attraction at the club. Hackman plays a pious "moral majority" conservative Senator from Ohio and Wiest his clueless homemaker wife. It won an Oscar for costume design and was nominated for art direction. Nathan Lane (one of the few to ever steal the spotlight from Williams) was nominated for a Golden Globe for Best Supporting Actor. The movie holds up well. But you can imagine the roar if it was made today and how many red states would attempt to ban it.

The LA Dodgers were set to honor the Sisters of Perpetual Indulgence, a historic LGBTQ service and charitable group, on the baseball club's Pride night in June. The Dodgers rescinded the honor under pressure from some notorious anti-LGBTQ bigots. The Dodgers then got tons of flak and restored the honor for the Sisters.

A Randy Rainbow video mocks Florida Govern DeSantis with frequent references to gay humor, including drag queens. Randy himself appears both as a man in a necktie and a woman in dresses.

In the small town of North Brookfield, Massachusetts, the issue has come close to my home. A married couple in that town failed in their effort to put a stop to the Rural Justice Network's Small Town Pride drag performance on the town common. They circulated a petition trying to recall two elected town officials and seeking to cancel the performance, complaining of "blatant support of immorality." Aided by the American Civil Liberties Union, the officials refused to cancel the event.

Back in the 1970s, some gay men seeking to strengthen our alliance with lesbians and other women took a closer look at drag entertainment and raised some important questions.

One of the men recalled this in a message to me:

> Perhaps most tellingly, we sincerely asked, "How did drag differ from blackface?" Wasn't drag parallel to this once popular practice of stage and screen—white men blackening their faces with burnt cork to create farcical imitations of black men in straw hats playing banjos? Or think of Al Jolson in heavy blackface singing "Mammy" in *The Jazz Singer*. Wasn't blackface correctly condemned for demeaning black people in much the same way as male drag demeans women? Blackface had been removed from entertainment spaces as having been an example of blatant racism. Why was drag still permitted?
>
> But beyond that, the specific public conduct of drag queens vis-a-vis women at that time truly deserved censure. These were the days when in New York City's gay clubs and bars drag queen performers continually offended with their negative attitudes towards women and the language they used to describe them. Drag acts won laughter and applause from their gay male audiences by continually making women the butt of their jokes. Common drag humor included calling women bitches, cunts, and fish, referring to women's supposedly smelly vaginas.

That friend and I had a conversation recently about the topic, and we agree that it is relatively rare for today's drag queens to carry on with such vulgar anti-women humor. We concluded that, for the most part, drag queens nowadays use costumes, wigs, exaggerated makeup, and often musical talent to entertain their audiences. They may even bore some audiences—as someone told me recently—but they have a lot of talent, a lot of nerve, and they can be quite funny, too. I can't imagine them hurting anyone except maybe another drag queen who tries to hide their makeup kit!

On a visit to a gay bar in Sarasota, Florida, last February, I met an elderly drag queen (that's a rarity) who went by the stage name Grandma Pearl. After singing, like many drag queens in gay bars, she wandered around accepting donations, and I chatted with her for a few minutes. Grandma Pearl told me that as a young man, he performed in the circus as a trapeze artist and clown, and that's what brought him to Sarasota decades ago.

Drag Queen Grandma Pearl chats with author Allen Young in a Sarasota, Florida, gay bar.
photo by David Malin

I'd like to end with a photo of my friend, the late John Burton, a gay man who liked to dress up in drag for parties, especially costume parties. He dressed as Marie Antoinette, queen of France, and if you look carefully in the headdress, you'll see it's a cage with a live white rat in it! Sometimes, John dressed as a rather lovely, though somewhat skinny, Miss Liberty.

John died of AIDS in 1991, but his memory lives on. I honor John as one of my friends who did good quality drag.

John Burton as Marie Antoinette
photo by Allen Young
published in the *Rag Blog*, theragblog.com

Solar Arrays Should Not Be Built Just Anywhere
2018

I'm a big fan of alternative energy. Clearly, it's time for humans to reduce and eventually eliminate the use of fossil fuels, as science has proven that climate change seriously threatens the planet.

There are various forms of alternative energy, including hydro from dammed rivers and wind, but the most rapidly growing is photovoltaic or solar energy. As solar arrays are being constructed in our region, it is time for a serious look at where they are being built and their overall impact.

Siting, quantity, and size of arrays are all issues to be considered, as well as their impact on the environment. Wise regulation of photovoltaic production must be developed and utilized.

The Athol Board of Planning and Community Development is required to act on an application from a solar developer to cover a portion of the eastern slope above Tully Lake with a solar array. The land, previously considered for a housing development but rejected after vocal opposition, is now owned by William Jardus Trustees, et. al, Edward C. Jardus Living Trust.

I submitted a written comment to the board. Here's what I submitted:

Please do whatever you can to stop the construction of a large solar array on the slope that goes down to Tully Lake from Chestnut Hill Avenue. As you know from previous hearings about the use of this land, large numbers of people do not want that slope degraded. Tully Lake Recreation Area is one of the most important public recreation areas in the entire region, attracting thousands of people annually—and more each year. People hiking and paddling in the Tully Lake area do not want to see an industrial installation, which is what a solar array is. They want to see green forests and blue sky and beautiful clean waterways.

We need solar energy production, but only in appropriate locations. This developer should not be allowed to degrade the Tully Lake Recreation Area. Many people, including me, have been involved in an effort to promote appreciation for our natural resources and to use these resources as a source of economic improvement through ecotourism. Please respect those efforts which have been growing and starting to yield results. Thank you.

Right now, another large solar array, having been given the green light by the Orange Planning Board, is under construction in West Orange, on a forested plateau northwest of the intersection of West Orange and Haskins roads. A sixty-acre healthy forest teeming with wildlife is being cut down to make way for solar panels. The developers have hired Orange forester Fred Heyes to cut down the trees.

While Fred and I agree on the benefits of "managed forestry," the West Orange endeavor has nothing to do with managed forestry. It is about destruction of the forest for another purpose, theoretically a good purpose, but many things are not taken into consideration such as the impact on wildlife, water quality, and carbon sequestration.

It is reasonable for any town, including Orange with its historic commitment to rural values, to limit the number of solar arrays within its borders. Sacrificing forest and farmland should not be without limits. While the Orange Planning Board and Orange Conservation Commission reviewed the plan and supposedly had no basis to stop it, board members could have issued a statement of concern—as they had every right to do. After all, the words "planning' and "conservation" have meaning!

Some of my feelings about the project are admittedly personal because I have seen my good friend Rice Flanders, 122 West Orange Road, crying her eyes out because she is losing that woodland behind her house that she has practically worshipped for more than four decades.

For full disclosure I need to mention that I am currently consuming electric power from a solar array in Rutland. I did it through Community Energy Solar, LLC, based in Radnor, Pennsylvania. I'm billed monthly and don't pay anything to National Grid unless I go over my average monthly consumption. I thus save money and support alternative energy at the same time.

The Rutland array is on six acres of a former hayfield, dubbed "retired farmland," and Community Solar's arrangement with the landowner calls for future dismantling of the solar equipment when it is no longer useful and allowing the land to be returned to other uses.

Finally, please don't call such industrial installations solar farms. They do not create food to eat. They manufacture power. Let's find a way to develop alternative energy not in a haphazard way, as is being done, but while caring, respecting, and conserving the land.

Published in *Athol Daily News*, June 14, 2018
Copyright © 2018 by Newspapers of Massachusetts, Inc.
Used with permission.
Update: No solar array went up on the slope above Tully Lake, and that land is now owned by the state for conservation.

Wheeler Mansion, Orange
photo by Allen Young

A Gilded-Age Mansion in Orange on Sale for $742,500
2015

The famed American writer Mark Twain coined the term Gilded Age for the late nineteenth-century era when fortunes were made and mansions were built.

Newport, Rhode Island, has a collection of mansions so large and famous that it has been a major tourist destination for decades. Fortunes made by capitalist industrialists in such fields as railroads and mining were tapped to hire the finest craftsmen and buy the most luxurious materials from around the world to build their houses.

In the North Quabbin region, there is only one mansion of that type, and it was built in 1902-1903 by John

Wheeler, who made his fortune manufacturing and selling sewing machines. He was the president of New Home Sewing Machine Company, located in most of the brick factory buildings along the Millers River in Orange. He died in 1910.

The house that Wheeler and his wife, Almira, built is located at 75 East Main Street, Orange, and went on the market with an asking price of $742,500. For much of the twentieth century, the building was owned by the Order of the Eastern Star, a Masonic sisterhood, serving as a home for elderly members.

Area residents who once belonged to groups such as the Girl Scouts have memories of visiting the home to entertain the residents. Hazel Lackey of Orange worked there for two decades as a cook. She said residents turned over all their assets to Eastern Star in exchange for their care.

Lee Lozier of Athol said,
> Twenty-five years ago, when I was fire chief in Orange, I had to conduct fire safety inspections, and I used to just admire the architecture as I made my way through the building. As old as the building was, it passed inspections.

The Eastern Star closed the place down in the 1980s, and it deteriorated somewhat until purchased in 1996 by the current owners, Karen and Robert Anderson. They bought it from the Star Realty Trust for $240,000, according to the Franklin County Registry of Deeds.

The Andersons originally planned to open a bed and breakfast under the name Anderson Manor, but those plans never materialized, according to Robert Anderson, primarily because the couple found themselves overtaken by other priorities—raising a family and caring for two ailing grandmothers.

He explained that a great deal of effort and money went into repairs and improvements in the building with its 15,406 square feet of living space. He recalled working for 12 hours to spray paint a decorative ceiling in the parlor room, using an artist's brush to spread the paint properly.

The listing broker is Stephanie Pandiscio of Foster-Healey Real Estate. The listing markets the house:

> From the brick and sandstone façade, the formal living room with elegant plasterwork, the carved mahogany dining room encircled with a continuous frieze depicting a hunting scene, to the library paneled in red birch and the den in quartered sycamore, this extraordinary property offers a once in a lifetime opportunity to own a piece of history. Many of the major spaces have been lovingly restored by the current owners and includes a state-of-the-art Buderus heating system. As a private residence, bed and breakfast, restaurant, wedding and event venue, corporate retreat, or other creative use, this masterpiece would have few equals.

In the real estate business, the well-known saying is "location, location, location," and the reality of downtown Orange—as much as we like to emphasize the positive aspects about our region—will make the sale of the property quite a challenge, according to many people, including real estate brokers I have spoken to.

Chuck Berube of Petersham, who specializes in high end residential property, calls it a "wonderful challenge," and since Pandiscio is a professional Realtor with lots of energy and creativity, there's a decent chance for a positive outcome.

As for the Andersons, after nineteen years in the building, where they were responsible stewards and even hosted Starry, Starry Night concerts, "the time is right to move on," as Robert Anderson put it.

Coincidentally, the Wheelers' so-called summer house at 123 Wheeler Avenue is also on the market with an asking price of $425,000. That house features beautiful Victorian-era woodwork and stained glass. The owner is Joan Raughtigan, widow of John Raughtigan, MD. The listing broker is Four Columns Realty.

Published in *Athol Daily News*, March 26, 2015
Copyright © 2015 by Newspapers of Massachusetts, Inc.
Used with permission.

Update: The Andersons stopped paying their mortgage and walked away from the building, and it was foreclosed. Then it deteriorated considerably and finally went back on the market. Cynthia "Sinde" Butler, then a resident of Los Angeles searching the internet for an interesting old building, eventually bought it in 2020 for $150,000. Since her purchase, she has put sweat equity and many dollars into bringing the building back from its near ruin. It is now available as a bed and breakfast and for special events such as weddings.

The Wheeler Avenue house has also been sold.

Allen Young, Cynthia "Sinde" Butler, and David Malin, from left, enjoy her fiftieth birthday party in the mansion.
photo courtesy of Cynthia Butler

Let's Reinvigorate the North Quabbin Bioreserve
2018

What is the North Quabbin Bioreserve? It was definitely something in 2002, and now it seems to be nothing but a memory shared by a very few people.

Those three words, North Quabbin Bioreserve, however, are engraved on a huge boulder not far from my home, and I visit it often.

The boulder is located just off Tully Road, several hundred yards south of its intersection with Butterworth Road in North Orange on the northwestern edge of the twelve-hundred-acre Tully Mountain Wildlife Management Area. If the North Quabbin Trails Association is successful in rerouting Tully Trail, it will include a spur trail to the boulder.

The placement of the boulder occurred on a cold December day in 2002 with participation of state officials, local landowners, and environmentalists including me, and staff of the Mount Grace Land Conservation Trust. Bob Durand, Massachusetts Secretary of Environmental Affairs, declared the creation of the bioreserve, and the boulder includes his name, that of Governor Jane Swift, and a dedication to landowners of the Tully River watershed. The West Branch of Tully River flows southward there, through a large scenic wetland called Tully Meadows.

At the dedication, Durand had just completed the Tully Initiative directing more than a million dollars in state funds to conserve nine thousand acres in the region via more than a hundred transactions—with the help of the Mount Grace Land Conservation Trust.

Speaking then, Durand said,
> Today, we are forever preserving one of the most pristine areas of Massachusetts, home to a wealth of plant and animal species, The North Quabbin Bioreserve will be a place where natural communities will continue to thrive and will serve as a place where people can enjoy nature, unspoiled.

The total area includes 55,000 acres of protected land within about 120,000 acres in 11 towns, plus another nearby 80,000 acres of Quabbin Reservation land.

The North Quabbin area was the second to receive the bioreserve dedication under Durand's leadership, the other being the Southeastern Massachusetts Bioreserve with fourteen thousand acres in Fall River, Freetown, and Dartmouth.

Durand said he first saw a bioreserve forest with millions of preserved acres in Russia, and it inspired him. He explained the concept was first developed by the United Nations Educational, Scientific, and Cultural Organization, UNESCO, as a way to protect large functioning, unfragmented ecosystems where natural communities can exist unhindered by development.

Actually, the UN terminology is somewhat different, labeling such areas as Biosphere Reserves. Created in 1971, UNESCO's Man and the Biosphere Program, according to UN documents,
> developed the basis for the sustainable use and conservation of biological diversity and for the improvement of the relationship between people and their environment globally. The

program encourages interdisciplinary research, demonstration and training in natural resource management.

I went on the internet to catch up on the status of the two bioreserves. I found nothing on any state website. A map showing the bioreserve outline, produced by the state long ago, is not available online. There were some outdated mentions of the bioreserves on websites maintained by private environmental groups, but that's it.

When informed of my concern, Leigh Youngblood, Mount Grace executive director, commented,

> At a minimum, the designation serves as a placeholder for an area worthy of further special investment. It would be nice to have a document of its specific history and conservation values, but someone or some entity would have to have a reason for prioritizing it.

The press liaison of the current state Executive Office of Environmental Affairs had no updated information, explaining only that

> one-time funding was allocated for land protection projects in these reserves. No funding has been allocated to protect land specifically in these 'bioreserves' since that point, but land conservation is a priority for the Baker-Polito administration.

Clearly, it's time to reinvigorate the North Quabbin Bioreserve. Let's all be proud that we live in a unique place acknowledged by the Commonwealth under a UN concept.

Our region's environment organizations–town conservation commissions plus Mount Grace, North Quabbin Trails Association, Athol Bird and Nature Club, Millers River Watershed Council—should all use the term North Quabbin Bioreserve and thus promote its goals.

I urged legislators Representative Susannah Whipps and Senator Anne Gobi to reach out to their colleagues who serve the towns of the Southeastern Bioreserve so that they can all work together to increase awareness and funding for the two bioreserves.

Local businesses from banks to real estate firms to restaurants and retail stores can help promote and honor the North Quabbin Bioreserve.

I'll end with the words of the man who created it. Durand was guest speaker at the annual meeting of Mount Grace in 2011 and spoke enthusiastically as he celebrated the tenth anniversary of the bioreserve. He told the members,

> You are protecting our valuable watersheds and wildlife habitat. It is important work because you enhance the working forests and farmlands of the North Quabbin. And it is important because you are leaving a lasting legacy for your children and their children.

Published in *Athol Daily News*, May 25, 2018
Copyright © 2018 by Newspapers of Massachusetts, Inc.
Used with permission.

Update: In the seven years since I wrote this column, nothing new has happened with regard to the state's two bioreserves.

Who Is Athol's Most Famous Native Son
2017

Only three years ago, our community was excited about Athol native Shawn Patterson, born 1965, whose song "Everything Is Awesome" in the Lego movie won an Academy Award. At that moment, with lots of media attention, he was the town's most famous native son. He's still my Facebook friend and continues to thrive and be creative in Los Angeles.

Another musician from Tooltown, David W. "Dave" Bargeron, born 1942, a trombonist and tuba player, became quite famous for playing with the jazz-rock group Blood, Sweat, and Tears. My research tells me he's still active. His website is davebargeron.com.

Charles R. Starrett, 1903–1986, often comes to mind as a famous Atholite. A grandson of L.S. Starrett, founder of the tool company, Charles was best known for his starring role in more than a hundred Durango Kid western series films.

Then there's Ginery Twichell (1811 – 1883). I remember when the Twichell Fountain in uptown Athol was in the news a couple of decades ago. There was talk of moving it downtown adjacent to the Athol Savings Bank, but that plan was soon scuttled. That's when I learned about the stagecoach operator for the Worcester to Brattleboro line for whom the fountain is named.

When he was done with being a stagecoach driver, he became president of the Boston and Worcester Railroad in the 1860s, Republican Representative in the US Congress for Massachusetts for three consecutive terms, and sixth president of the Atchison, Topeka, and Santa Fe Railway.

But my choice for Athol's most famous native individual is Lysander Spooner,1808 -1887. His extensive *Wikipedia* page describes him as

> an American individualist anarchist, political philosopher, essayist, pamphlet writer, Unitarian abolitionist, supporter of the labor movement, legal theorist, and entrepreneur of the nineteenth century.

There is a website dedicated to him, lysanderspooner.org.

I first learned about this remarkable man from local historian Dick Chaisson. His tribute to Spooner, entitled "The Man Who Challenged the US Post Office," was published in *Hometown Chronicles,* the book by Chaisson that I published via Millers River Publishing Company in 1985. That book is out of print but available on the internet used book market.

Spooner was upset about the high cost of mailing letters, so he set up the American Letter Mail Company, but it was found to be in violation of federal law.

In his account, originally printed in the Worcester's Telegram & Gazette newspaper, Chaisson quotes Athol historian Lilley B. Caswell who writes that Spooner "was undoubtedly the most unique and remarkable character Athol ever produced."

Spooner grew up on a farm on Petersham Road and became a lawyer without going to law school. He favored self-employment and decried government licensing as against individual liberty. His most famous writing includes the seminal abolitionist book *The Unconstitutionality of Slavery and No Treason: The Constitution of No Authority,* which opposed treason charges against secessionists. In recent years, Spooner has been a hero to libertarians and right-wing political elements, but his views have appeal to left-wing anarchists, too. Like Thomas Jefferson, Spooner was a deist and wrote essays very critical of Christianity.

Chaisson quotes John Boyle O'Reilly, the so-named poet sage of Boston, eulogizing Lysander Spooner upon his death in 1887: "He was one of the greatest men the world ever saw . . . even a greater man than Ralph Waldo Emerson."

I credit Larry Buell of Petersham for encouraging me to write about Spooner, in part because Larry has taken the persona of Lysander's cousin, Lucius Spooner, a Petersham farmer and millwright who kept a journal in the 1840s. Buell, costumed as Lucius Spooner, gives talks on local history and environmental protection.

Like me, Buell is drawn to the concept of a sense of place, and we share our affection for the North Quabbin region and a desire to promote the region as a unique place worthy of both celebration and protection. People like Lysander Spooner are part of that proud heritage.

Published in *Athol Daily News,* March 30, 2017
Copyright © 2017 by Newspapers of Massachusetts, Inc.
Used with permission.
Update: A historic plaque on a boulder is located roadside near the house at 559 Petersham Road, Athol, where Lysander Spooner once lived. Trombonist Dave Bargeron died January 18, 2025.

Ethel Rosenberg's Life Story Told in New Book
2021

COLD SPRING, New York—On June 19, 1953, the government of the United States of America, utilizing its much-heralded but deeply-flawed system of justice, ended the lives of Julius and Ethel Rosenberg. They were put to death that day in the electric chair at Sing Sing Prison on the banks of the Hudson River.

The atrocious action was, in my view, the most egregious moment in the long, dark period of mid-twentieth-century America combining the Cold War and related anti-Communist crusade often called the McCarthy Era.

Ethel Greenglass (later Rosenberg) in 1961 as she graduated from Seward High School in New York City.
photo courtesy of Michael and Robert Meeropol and the Rosenberg Fund for Children

The Rosenberg case has been the topic of many books, and I highly recommend the newest one, *Ethel Rosenberg: An American Tragedy* written by Anne Sebba, an award-winning biographer, lecturer, and former Reuters foreign correspondent. She is a senior research fellow at the Institute of Historical Research in London, where she resides. I found the book interesting and well-written, though painfully sad at times due to the injustice and cruelty of the execution. Focusing primarily but not exclusively on Ethel makes the book unique.

Various segments in the 309-page volume provide historic context quite well, and I find that valuable, given the passage of so many decades. She writes that the oral indictment read out in court deliberately described the crime as having been committed during the early years of the Cold War, even though the arrest and trial technically occurred in peacetime. Yet, amid the bloody stalemate in Korea and the frenzied building of nuclear fallout shelters around New York City, Ethel and Julius were cast as traitors who had helped Stalin steal the secure future that most Americans believed they had won in 1945.

More about the book later, but for the sake of full disclosure, I want to point out that I have been familiar with the Rosenberg case ever since my childhood as a red diaper baby. I was twelve when they were executed, and I remember clearly my parents' deeply felt concern and grief. And no wonder! The Rosenbergs and Youngs were not that different—all four were the children of Jewish immigrants from Eastern Europe and also immersed in the American and international Communist movement.

Even more significant is the fact that I met the two Rosenberg sons, Michael and Robert, only five years after their parents' execution. It was due to a coincidence, as friends of my family happened to reside in an uptown Manhattan apartment building across the hall from Anne and Abel Meeropol, adopted parents of the boys. Anne and Abel thought that a Columbia College freshman with leftist parents, namely me, would be a good friend for Michael, a high school junior. Michael and I have remained good friends ever since that time, and I recently visited him at his home in Cold Spring, New York, which is why that's the dateline for this book review.

Michael Meeropol, left, and Robert Meeropol at the White House
photo by Alan Heath • courtesy of the Rosenberg Fund for Children

In another odd coincidence, while driving from Cold Spring to Croton-on-Hudson, New York, to visit a cousin, I passed through Ossining, the town where the Sing

Sing prison is located—and still open for business. In another coincidence, Croton-on-Hudson has a reputation for almost a century as a New York City suburb of choice for leftists, including left-wing journalist John Reed, whose Croton home is featured in the award-winning movie *Reds*.

Regardless of an individual's familiarity with the Rosenberg case, *Ethel Rosenberg: An American Tragedy* is worth reading. It does a fine job telling the story of the complex espionage case against the young couple while also going into a lot of detail about Ethel as a wife and mother. For example, she loved to sing and had some knowledge of opera, and her talent and interest in the arts could have taken her on a very different pathway were it not also for the leftist politics embraced by many New York Jews from the 1920s into following decades.

This book review is not the place to elaborate on the complexity of the real espionage that occurred in the 1940s and the long cast of characters that included not only Julius Rosenberg but also Ethel's brother David Greenglass. The testimony of Greenglass was key for the prosecution's case, and Sebba explains the legalities and illegalities well, including the use of intimidation and perjured testimony.

The Jewish identity of the Rosenbergs is another aspect that Sebba covers with sensitivity and insight. I assume the author is Jewish. I don't know this for a fact, but *Wikipedia* says that her maiden name is Rubenstein. I, too, am Jewish—my mother's maiden name is Goldfarb.

Roy Cohn, then a young recent law school graduate and a staunchly anti-communist Jew, played a role in helping Jewish prosecutor Irving Saypol bring the case before a Jewish judge, Irving Kaufman. That made it less likely that the Jewish community would rally around the Rosenbergs, though many Jews could not help but link the very idea of electrocution to the recent reality of the Nazi ovens.

Ethel's identity as a woman is woven throughout Sebba's narrative, sometimes to excess with reference to her wardrobe and makeup and the impact they may have had on jurors. The prosecution knew that there could be a problem in executing a young mother and orphaning two children, and it is very clear from the facts as we know them now that Ethel was in fact innocent of the charges against her. The prosecution thought they could coerce her to name names or compel her husband to do so, but she had steely resolve and would not surrender.

There were even absurd theories put forward by some individuals that Ethel was a mastermind. President Dwight Eisenhower, who declined to grant clemency shortly before the execution took place, is one of those who took up the idea, describing Ethel as "the more strong-minded and apparent leader of the two." The author's use of relevant quotations, such as that one, enriches the book throughout.

Sebba interviewed many people, including the Rosenberg sons, and for me, given my friendship with Michael as well as with Robby, it led to some deep sadness as I read. The boys—who both have fared very well as adults with their family and professional lives—

went through hell when they were so young. The photo of them, accompanied by defense attorney Manny Bloch bringing them to visit their parents in Sing Sing, is enough to bring tears to my eyes and probably to others' as well.

Attorney Bloch, aided by his father, worked very hard to provide a vigorous defense. As one might expect, there are people who think a more experienced or better known lawyer should have taken the case. The Rosenbergs were sympathizers of the Communist Party, and perhaps one or both were members, but the Party leadership apparently concluded it was best for it to remain in the background lest it do harm to the defendants.

Clearly, however, the international Communist movement, especially in Western Europe, brought many people to the streets to protest the execution of an innocent couple.

Maintaining the innocence of both Rosenbergs as well as of their co-defendant Morton Sobell, was the focus of political activism before and after their execution. However, after the fall of the Berlin Wall in 1989, documents located in the Soviet Union showed that Julius was indeed an agent working for the Russians. Late in life after serving a long prison sentence, Sobell acknowledged some guilt. A crucial point is that Julius's communication with Soviet operatives took place during World War II when the Soviets were vital allies in the battle against Nazism and fascism and could best be described as "industrial espionage."

The prosecution maintained that the "secret of the atomic bomb" was given to the Russians by the Rosenbergs. That was a very big lie, as Russian scientists had all the information they needed from other sources to make a bomb. Those Russian documents make it clear, in various ways, that Ethel was totally innocent.

In the early 1970s, Michael and Robby, who had not been open about their identity, came out as the Rosenbergs as a lawsuit was filed against Louis Nizer for his book quoting their parents' copyrighted letters without permission. Around that time, I was teaching a course on the 1950s at Tufts University's extension program, and Michael's very first public appearance as Rosenberg was in front of my class.

The article on the Rosenberg case in *Wikipedia* states:
> Their sons' current position is that Julius was legally guilty of the conspiracy charge, though not of atomic spying, while Ethel was only generally aware of his activities. The children say that their father did not deserve the death penalty and that their mother was wrongly convicted. They continue to campaign for Ethel to be posthumously legally exonerated.

Sebba helps the reader with the historic context:
> Both Ethel and Julius were charged under the Espionage Act of 1917 with conspiracy to commit espionage from 1944 until 1950 by communicating to a foreign government, in wartime, secret atomic and other military information. The time period was significant. Their last alleged overt act relating to atomic secrets was in mid-September 1945, but World War Two officially ended on September 2, 1945. However, other aspects of the conspiracy continued into 1950.

There was a concerted effort in the final years of Barack Obama's presidency to have Ethel fully exonerated, but he did not exonerate her, a great disappointment to the brothers and their supporters.

Sebba does a fine job of including moving and insightful information in her book about the adoptive parents, Anne and Abel Meeropol, and of Michael and Robby and their families. My review of an outstanding movie about Roy Cohn, directed by Michael's daughter Ivy Meeropol, was published after I saw its debut screening at the New York Film Festival. If you haven't seen that film, you should find it on HBO or perhaps elsewhere. It includes references to the Rosenberg case, of course.

Ethel Rosenberg: An American Tragedy includes many photographs, some from the private collection of the Meeropol brothers. It also includes numerous quotations from the media, and I want to offer just one. After the trial and the imposition of the death sentence, Sebba writes, "the crusading columnist Dorothy Thompson had been almost alone among reporters in writing that the death sentence was too harsh." And she offers this from Thompson:

> Treason in our times has somehow escaped satisfactory legal definition. Treason has hitherto been equated to betrayal to an enemy with whom the country is in armed conflict. Only because the Rosenbergs gave secret information to a foreign power in 1944, in wartime, could Judge Kaufman impose the formidable sentence. But in 1944 we were not at war with the Soviet Union. The Soviets were not an enemy but an ally. In 1944 Julius and Ethel Rosenberg were in their twenties, for three years the Soviet Union had been glorified by the most responsible citizens. The prevailing myths, hopes and policies all contributed to create the climate in which their crime might seem to them hardly more than misdemeanor. Indeed, it is unlikely that had they been tried in 1944 they would have received any such sentence.

Whether you read the book or not, I urge *Rag Blog* readers to learn more about the Rosenberg Fund for Children, RFC, and if you are so inclined, make a donation. Back in the 1950s and beyond, people throughout the world who felt that the execution of the Rosenbergs was a terrible injustice contributed money to help secure a safe future for the Rosenberg boys. Those orphans were so lucky to end up with the Meeropols as their adopted parents, though there were some rough months before the final legal action took place for their adoption.

Robby Meeropol was aware of that aspect of his own past and also not entirely satisfied with his previous career as a lawyer, so he founded and led the charity to raise money to provide help for children of modern-day activists. As people had helped him have a good life, the RFC helps children of parents working on behalf of the environment, racial justice, peace, lesbian and gay rights, and more. That charity, now led by Robby's daughter Jennifer Meeropol provides funding for such things as music lessons, summer camp, and counseling, At RFC.org, you can learn more and perhaps make a donation.

I want to end this book review by stating that the injustice in the Rosenberg case is just one reason that the death penalty should be abolished under federal law and in those states that still allow it. I shudder at the thought of that intentional taking of a human life in my name, as a citizen of this republic. It still goes on despite evidence that innocent people have been killed.

Massachusetts, where I live, no longer has the death penalty, and yet there is an organization in my state that opposes the death penalty. Why? Because it's a fact that many people endorse it and could advocate for its return.

If you like movies, especially old movies, look for *I Want to Live* starring Susan Hayward. Released in 1958, it is a very moving drama based on a true story about a woman sentenced to death. I have a vivid memory of the day I saw that movie. I was a college student, age seventeen alone in a theater in New York City not far from my Columbia University dormitory. I had a strong emotional response to the movie, and I know deep in my heart that feeling related to the Rosenberg case, so fresh in my mind, as that year I met Michael Meeopol. I was so upset that I decided to board a subway train and take the longest possible subway ride—out to Far Rockaway and back—close to two hours spent deep in mournful thought and outrage about the very idea of the state killing people.

Reading Sebba's informative book brought back that same emotion.

published in the *Rag Blog*, theragblog.com

Appreciating Nature as a Political Act
2020

Do you consider yourself an environmentalist? Dictionary.com has this definition: "A person who is concerned with or advocates the protection of the environment." That definition suits me, and I assume it's valid for all or most *Rag Blog* readers.

I belong to some local and national environmental groups, and I've attended demonstrations over many years related to the dangers of nuclear power and the fossil fuel industry's expansion of pipelines. I've become informed about the danger of climate change and the need to respond to it. I also choose candidates with strong commitment to environmental protection.

Being an environmentalist is made more authentic through my membership in a local land conservation trust and my day-to-day enjoyment of the natural world. Being outside in nature, taking a walk or a hike, perhaps paddling or pedaling are some of the most fulfilling things that we can do, especially in the midst of this pandemic.

Land conservation trusts exist nationwide, with lots of them in Texas, where *Rag Blog* is published. The one I belong to serves north central and western Massachusetts and is named after one of our prominent geological features. It is the Mount Grace Land Conservation Trust, and its website is illustrative.

The essay that follows was published on the front page of the Trust's newsletter. While it is about my experience and attitude toward Nature in the area where I live, I think it will be meaningful for *Rag Blog* readers, and if you are not already a land trust member, now would be a good time to join—and enjoy!

A Nature-Lover But Not a Naturalist

Walking on a country road or hiking on a forested trail are my favorite things to do these days, a good activity given the threat of COVID-19. I enjoy saying that I am a nature lover but not a naturalist. I am satisfied with my casual non-scientific way of observing and appreciating what my senses reveal to me during my time outdoors—and at home, too, just staring out the windows of my house or lounging on the deck watching the trees sway in the wind (or remain amazingly still), taking in the blueness of the sky and the shapes of the clouds, and at night checking out the moon and the stars.

I've been wanting to get to know Marielena Lima, Mount Grace communications and engagement coordinator. We decided to take a hike together, so we met at Mount Grace headquarters, ambled through the Skyfields Arboretum, and crossed the property line onto trails within Lawton State Forest. As we chatted, real examples of my attitude toward nature surfaced. We heard birdsong and were quiet for a few minutes as we listened. I did not say, "It's a wood thrush," because I simply don't know birdsong (except maybe a crow). I do know some amazing birders I've met through my involvement in the Athol Bird and Nature Club, and being with them on a hike enriches the experience. But I don't need the experts to enjoy birdsong.

The late Elizabeth Farnsworth conducted a fern workshop sponsored by Mount Grace in Royalston about a decade ago. I attended the session and paid full attention as she named more than a dozen kinds of ferns and described their traits, and I had a good time, but as I told Marielena when we saw many of those lush, beautiful plants on our walk, they are just unnamed ferns to me now.

I have my list of go-to people for questions about nature. For example, on our walk I pointed to some mushrooms and mentioned that my neighbor Rob Jalbert knows a lot about mushrooms and when I'm in the woods with him, he names them and declares which ones are edible.

Marielena and I saw some flowers as our walk drew to a close on Willis and Old Keene roads. First was a small wetland filled with water lilies. For fun, I later looked up the

wetland with water lilies
photo by Allen Young

Latin name, *Nymphaeaceae*, which I certainly won't remember! And then we stopped and smelled some white and pink flowers on a shrub that I could not identify, but I sent a

Meadowsweet
photo by Allen Young

photo to Rob who, with his great collection of field guides and apps, identified it as *Spiraea Alba*—common name, meadowsweet.

Finally, right across from Skyfields, I noticed a very large deciduous tree that I could not identify, though I enjoyed staring up at it curiously for a few minutes. I confidently can identify oak, maple, beech, and birch, but what was this stately tree? It's an ash, according to Kim Lynn Nguyen, Mount Grace stewardship manager.

previously published in the *Rag Blog*, theragblog.com

Acknowledgements

Many people were helpful to me as I worked on *From the Octagon*.

I am especially grateful for the financial support of ten sponsors who provided funds to help cover the cost of production and keep the cover price reasonable. Thanks go out to Althea Bramhall, Realtor; Lisa Carey, CPA; Jeff Cole of Witty's Funeral Home; Emma Ellsworth of Mount Grace Land Conservation Trust; Marcia Gagliardi of Haley's Antiques and Publishing; Peter Gerry of Pete's Tire Barn; Steve Goldsher, DDS, of Pioneer Valley Periodontics; Morris Housen of Erving Paper Mill; Brian Stoddard of Cornerstone Insurance; Dan Zona of Athol Savings Bank.

From the Octagon is a collaborative effort, and I am grateful to Marcia Gagliardi of Haley's for her expertise as publisher while Debra Ellis assisted as copy editor.

Choosing a limited number of articles from hundreds of possibilities was difficult, and I received help from Rice Flanders and Sally Howe.

Shawn Palmer, publisher of the *Athol Daily News* via Newspapers of Massachusetts, Inc., readily granted permission for use of previously published material as did Alice Embree, associate editor of the *Rag Blog*.

Thanks to Mike Phillips for the cover photograph, originally taken by him to help publicize my autobiography.

When I was writing my column for the *Athol Daily News,* editor Deb Porter and her successor Anita Fritz were helpful and encouraging. A longtime writer friend Katya Taylor often helped by "tweaking" articles when I sent her first drafts.

Lee Gutkopf and Justin Hughes of Tech One Computers know how to fix computers, and I'm grateful that they fixed mine when needed.

When I called upon my neighbors at Butterworth Farm—Jerry Marcanio, Rob Jalbert, and David Spackman—to assist me with difficult chores, they showed up and pitched in.

Finally, my life partner of forty-five years, David Malin, provided encouragement, support, love, and companionship, as well as contributing energy and creativity to my daily life and surroundings in the Octagon House.

Allen Young

About the Author

Allen Young has lived in Royalston, Massachusetts, since 1973, coming with several friends to the North Quabbin region of central Massachusetts as part of the back-to-the-land movement. He helped build his own octagonal timber-framed house, has hiked and canoed throughout the region, and has cultivated a productive organic vegetable garden.

He first experienced forests, waterfalls, and gardening during his childhood on a poultry farm in the foothills of the Catskill Mountains in New York state, where he was born in 1941. After graduating from Fallsburgh Central High School, he attended Columbia

College in New York City, receiving the bachelor of arts degree in 1962. He earned a master of arts degree in Hispanic-American and Luso-Brazilian studies from Stanford University in California and a master of science degree from the Columbia University Graduate School of Journalism.

Upon receiving a Fulbright Scholarship in 1964, he spent three years in Brazil and other Latin American countries, and while there he contributed numerous articles to the New York Times, the Christian Science Monitor, and other periodicals.

Returning to the United States in 1967, he worked briefly as a reporter for the Washington Post, resigning in the fall of that year to become a full-time antiwar activist and staff member of Liberation News Service.

In 1970, following the Stonewall Rebellion in New York City, Young participated in the gay liberation movement, collaborating with lesbian writer and scholar Karla Jay on four books, including the pioneering anthology *Out of the Closets: Voices of Gay Liberation*.

After returning to his rural roots, Young became a reporter for the *Athol Daily News*, later serving as assistant editor. He launched Millers River Publishing Company in 1983 to produce his regional guidebook *North of Quabbin* and published more than a dozen titles after that. Haley's published his *North of Quabbin Revisited* in 2003.

From 1989 to 1999, he was director of community relations for Athol Memorial Hospital. He was a co-founder of the North Quabbin Diversity Awareness Group. In 1998, he was the first recipient of the North Quabbin Community Coalition's Barbara Corey Award "in honor of his passion for life, his values and his love for the citizens of our region." In 2004, he received the Writing and Society Award from the University of Massachusetts English Department "honoring a distinguished career of commitment to the work of writing in the world."

He was invited by Erving Paper Mills to write the official company history for its 2005 centennial. Other books of local interest include *Millers River Reader*, which he edited; *Make Hay While the Sun Shines: Farms, Forests, and People of the North Quabbin; The Man Who Got Lost: North Quabbin Stories;* and *Thalassa: One Week in a Provincetown Dune Shack.*

He self-published his autobiography, *Left, Gay & Green: A Writer's Life,* in 2018.

Colophon

Text for *From the Octagon* is set in Century Schoolbook, a modern serif typeface designed by Morris Fuller Benton in 1924. It was originally designed to be an easy-to-read font for use in textbooks. Many Americans first learned to read with books set in Century Schoolbook, which can give the typeface a pleasant, nostalgic feeling.

Titles and captions are set in Gill Sans, a classic British humanist sans-serif typeface designed by Eric Gill in the 1920s. Gill Sans is known for clean, modern lines inspired by Roman and pen-written letterforms. It features a distinctive double-story lowercase g, a perfect circular O, and specific stroke details like flat-topped lowercase d, p, and q. With a wide range of weights, Gill Sans is versatile, suitable for both traditional text and bold display use, and has become an enduring and ubiquitous presence in British design and media.

www.ingramcontent.com/pod-product-compliance
Lightning Source LLC
Chambersburg PA
CBHW062002220426
43662CB00010B/1209